Paramount Gift Books

What the Quran Says About Itself

Prof. Muhammad Rafi

What the Quran Says About Itself

by

Prof. Muhammad Rafi

First Edition 2014

Paramount Books (Pvt) Ltd.

152/O, Block-2, P.E.C.H.S., Karachi-75400, Pakistan
Tel: 34310030, Fax: 34553772, E-mail: paramount@cyber.net.pk
Website: www.paramountbooks.com.pk

ISBN: 978-969-637-022-2
Printed in Pakistan

INTRODUCTION

Mankind practises different religions. Some of them are Divinely revealed, while others are not. Man-made religions' are an abomination before Allah and will never succeed in the long run. The Quran terms 'Islam' as 'Deen' (way of leading life positively). It is not a religion in the sense we use the term. The Arabic word 'Islam' simply means submission and derives from a word meaning 'peace'. In a religious context, it means complete submission to the will of Allah. The directives and guidance of the Almighty are preserved for all times in the Quran which is the last and final of the revealed books. Muhammad ﷺ is the last Messenger of Allah on to whom the Quran was revealed.

Quran is the only source and religious book in the world in which Allah addresses mankind in the first person (We, Us, Our). This booklet uses the term Allah instead of the commonly used term 'God' as the Quran also does so. The Quran helps us in understanding the infinite Might and Authority.

The self-confidence of the Quran is unprecedented. The language of the Quran is so confident and assertive that both believers and dis-believers have no choice but to acknowledge its extraordinary character and greatness as a book of guidance. The Quran guides mankind to immortality, gives them hope and saves them from leading a life devoid of meaning. It values our conviction that results from full mental acceptance and intellectual satisfaction

It is heartening to note that gradually the worth of this great book is being understood and the importance of understanding it is being emphasized. Sometimes even educated people complain that they cannot understand Quran from prevalent translations available in the market and the situation with tafaseer (commentaries) is such that the more you explain the more you lose the focus. This makes the younger generation nervous, and confused as to what to do. The height of their interest is reflected in the practice of reciting the Qur'an repeatedly but they do not comprehend what they recite. Their devotion and excitement leads them to recite one-fourth or half of a section (chapter), beyond which the reader loses interest to continue.

The truth is that the translation of the Qur'an, it may be in any language of the world, cannot explain the Qur'anic meanings.

A careful consideration of the situations in which such terms have been used in the Quran will amply demonstrate how the Divine message gets circumscribed by using these terms in their usual, constricted sense, whereas their broad construction expands the Quranic meaning beyond any limit.

The Glossary of Quranic terms has been given in detail in the booklet to help the readers understand the context and meaning of the verse (Ayat),

The promises made in the Quran are eventually to our benefit. This gives man an inner feeling of 'Amun' or peace.He can truly be called an Allah conscious person (Muttaqi). For this achievement Allah shall be pleased with him and reward him in this world as well as the hereafter. It is the moral, ethical and religious obligation of every Muslim to read, study, understand and apply the permanent values of the Quran in his life.

The verses in this book will be of great help in solving all our problems. It is incumbent upon a Muslim to search the Quran for the right path and solution to all of his problems. Only then our lives shall be truly peaceful and heavenly. The Quran is a unique testament of eternal truth and ever-abiding universal values that are meant for all times and all aspects of human life. Its teachings are never out of date, and there is no limit beyond which it could fail to enlighten and guide us. The Quran gives the spiritual commandments and laws through which man can live in peace and harmony with himself and his fellow creatures. It leads to an inner awakening and more positive approach to the values of life. Unlike other religions, it does not negate the study of nature. In fact it encourages the search for truth amidst the grandeur, beauty and mystery of the universe; and to a greater understanding of the primordial force and authority, which is responsible for what we see and feel around us. Above all we are not expected to follow the Quran blindly

"Clear proofs have come to you from your Rabb to open your eyes. Whosoever will make use of his sight (to understand), he will do so for his own good; and whoso behaves like a blind person will do so to his own harm' (6:104)

"We sent down in the Quran that which is a healing and a mercy for those who believe and to the unjust nothing but loss after loss" (17:82)

The whole corpus of Islamic principles is contained in the Quran. Quran is the best Hadith of Allah[39:23] and that of the Nabi[69:40-46].

The Almighty's final message to mankind is present in the Quran. Whatever principles, laws, injunctions and directives the Creator of this universe wished to convey for the enrichment and growth of our personalities were communicated to

His last and final Messenger ﷺ. The only course left to mankind to regain the lost paradise is to follow and practically apply these principles and values as was done by the exalted Messenger Muhammad (SAW). Consequently Allah's blessings will undoubtedly be showered on all those who benefit from these teachings and guidance.

"Allah has bound Himself to shower His blessings on those who believe in His Ayats and act accordingly." (6:54)

Human intellect is not aware of any source of knowledge other than itself. Consequently all it has offered has been relative to and bound by time and situation. In our world today, we find that man possesses wealth, power and vast resources. His wealth of knowledge, technical progress and control over the forces of nature is indeed astounding. What then is the cause of his discontent and the decline? The Quran provides us with an answer. The cause is within man himself.

'Allah never changes the condition of a nation until they first change what is in themselves (8:53)

There is only one guidance left for mankind that confidently proclaims its ability to lead humanity to its ultimate goal:

"The God that has created all the objects in the universe has also undertaken to make them aware of their goal and guide them towards it" (20:50)

The Quran explains itself at many places and tells us how and when it can be used as our guide :

1. It is a code of life and removes doubts of all kinds (2:2).
2. Everything revealed to the exalted Messenger Muhammad (SAW) is in it (6:19)
3. Muslims are ordered to obey it and not to obey anything else (7:3).
4. The exalted Messenger Muhammad (SAW) was also asked to follow it (10:109) and he took all his decisions according to it (5:48)
5. Those who do not decide their affairs according to the Quran are the ones who are 'Kaafireen' (Disbelievers and rejecters) 5:44
6. The Quran is the final revelation and no one is authorized to make any changes in it (6:34)
7. The Quran confirms and preserves the earlier Divine Revelations (5:48)
8. There is nothing contradictory in the Quran (4:82).
9. Whatever has been revealed in the Quran has been explained in it (75:19). This has been done by cross-references and repetition of Ayats called'Tasreef-e-Ayaat'(60:106, 17:41).
10. The Quran is the guiding light (5:15) and has been revealed so that human beings may

live their lives according to its teachings. (6:123)

11. The Quran ordains mankind to think and do research (47:24).
12. It is easy to get guidance from the Quran (54:16). At the same time it is necessary that the one seeking guidance should keep his mind clear and un-prejudiced (56:79).
13. The Quran has everything that is required for guidance: 'And We have revealed the Book to you which has the clear explanation of everything and is guidance and mercy and good news for those who submit'(16:89)
14. The Quran is a Book in which the verses are distinctly elucidated (41:3) 'Thus We make the Revelation distinct for a people who reflect' (10:24). Nothing is omitted from it (6:38).

This booklet mainly deals with what the Quran says about itself.The Ayaats in this collection will help all those who seek guidance from them. The Quran is the final authority in matters relating to the ways life should be lived. The principles and values in it form the cornerstone of the Islamic polity. It is a book of guidance for the whole of mankind and transcends the barriers of time and space.

Surah(Chapter) and Ayat (Verse) numbers have been given for the benefit of readers to have a comprehensive and contextual understanding of the Quranic directives. For example, 2:159 refers to the 2nd Surah (Al-Baqarah) Ayat number 159.

Some of the basic principles of guidance have been given below in nutshell as an example of Quran's greatness in understanding human nature and guiding us on the right path.

53:38 No laden one shall bear the load of another.

53:39 Every human being shall be responsible for his own works and compensated for his labour.

53:40 His effort (and not the results) will be seen.

53:41 Then he will be fully rewarded for it.

53:42 To your Sustainer (Rabb) is the final destination. [79:44. Your goal shall be your Lord's Rule on earth]

53:43 He is the One Who causes you to laugh, and to cry. [The basic principles that cause nations to live in prosperity versus misery, are being mentioned here]

53:44 He is the One Who gives death and gives life. [The rise and fall of nations follow His laws. And these laws are most excellently expounded in the Quran]

53:45 He is the One Who creates the two companions, the male and the female (pairs and opposites among His creation),

53:46 From gametes that unite.

53:47 He has promised to bring about a second life (the ultimate accountability).

53:48 He is the One Who gives wealth and contentment (according to His laws).

53:49 He is the One Who is the Sustainer (Rabb) of the brightest star*, the human intellect.

53:50 He is the One Who annihilated the former tribe of 'Aad. [They were men of intellect but refused to establish the Divine System. Allah never changes His laws, therefore, a wrong system, however smartly run, is bound to collapse]

*[Shi'ra = Sha'oor = Intellect. Shi'ra is also the Arabic name of the brightest star Sirius in the constellation Canis Major. It was widely worshiped in ancient Middle East]

GLOSSARY OF TERMS USED IN THE QURAN

1. Aaron/Harun/Haroon – Aaron was the elder brother of Moses. Both the brothers were Nabis (messengers)
2. Abraham/Ibrahim – Father of Ishmael and Isaac and grandfather of Jacob, was the first in the line of Anbiya (Messengers) sent to the people of Arabia
3. Adl – (Ain, Dal, Lam) means 'justice', but not merely the justice dispensed by a court of law; it covers justice in all spheres of life. Justice signifies the condition where every individual gets what is due to him. 'Due' means not only what is due to him economically but all the fundamental rights that belong to him by virtue of his being a human being.

4. Ajal – (alif-jeem-lam) Allah never destroys a nation unless it brings destruction upon itself through its own-wrongdoing. The messengers of Allah came to them and were ridiculed and refuted. Refusal to change their ways resulted in those nations creating social ills and imbalance and they were ultimately destroyed. According to the above law, the time gap between an action and the manifestation of its result is a period of respite termed as 'Ajal'
5. Aleem – (ain-lam-meem) Ilm means knowledge, to know something positively, to recognize, to find reality to the extent of certainty, to feel, to find out definitely (Taj/Moheet). One who knows these things in this process is called aalim (learned person), and its plural is aalimoon. Aalim (plural Ulama) is one whose knowledge is very deep,
6. Allah – (alif-lam-ha) This is the proper name of Allah (Al-llah), and all other names denote His various attributes. Ilah, by definition, is one: to whom someone looks for protection in bewilderment, by whose grandeur one gets dazed, whose overall sovereignty and ultimate authority is accepted, whose laws and commandments are obeyed and followed, and who is at the highest pedestal and remains unseen (Taj). Keeping in view

the above attributes, the name 'Allah' as it appears in the Quran would mean a Being Who is supreme but remains hidden from human eyes; before whose dignity and grandeur human perceptions become dazed; whose sovereignty extends over the entire universe; whose obedience is mandatory. By accepting Him as 'Ilah', one must accept only His sovereignty and obey His laws. The human mind just cannot perceive Him in any shape or physical form nor can it explain Him. He is beyond human perceptions (6:104). Nothing is like Him (42:11). However, we can explain His attributes as mentioned in the Quran. To believe in Allah would, therefore, mean to acknowledge and accept His sovereignty with all His attributes, as mentioned in the Quran, in the most balanced and proportionate manner (17:110. It is, incorrect to say that the Allah of all religions is the same that Rama or Raheem is one and the same thing. The Holy Father of Christians, the Yahweh of Jews, the Ishwar or Parmatma of Hindus and Armazd of Zoroastrians are totally different from each other – as their attributes are different from those of Allah as defined in the Quran. He is above all such perceptions! He cannot be transformed out of stone or a log of wood. The correct concept of Allah can only be perceived by explaining His attributes as narrated in the Quran, since only the Quran is exalted from the interplay of human thought. It is because of this reason that the Quran does not accept the existence of Allahs, which various people, tribes, or religions have carved out of their own thoughts.

7. Anbiya – The plural form of nabi – see nabi.
8. Bani-Israel – (literally, 'the children of Israel'). Jacob (Yaqoob) was the grandson of Abraham. His title was Israel, which means 'man of Allah'. His descendants are known as the Bani-Israel His fourth son was Yahuda or Judea whose tribe settled in Palestine. From this reference, this tribe came to be known as Jew (Yahud) and the remaining tribes as the Bani-Israel
9. Deen – (dal-ya-noon) This word has been used in various forms and meanings, e.g. power, supremacy, ascendancy, sovereignty or lord ship, dominion, law, constitution, mastery, government, realm, decision, definite outcome, reward and punishment. On the other hand, this word is also used in the sense of obedience, submission and allegiance (Taj, Moheet). In the Holy

Quran this word is used in almost all the above meanings in as many as 79 verses. Ad-deen is to surrender before that supreme authority which provides nourishment to the entire universe and lays down the laws and the code (2:131–132). "The day of deen" is when no man has any power over another man and all the affairs of mankind. It would be decided according to the law of Allah. Verse (1:3) also gives reference to this day, period or stage of history when humankind would lead their lives according to the law of Allah. These laws of Allah in their final and complete form are given in the Quran, and are called ad-deen.

10. Eiman/Iman/momin/momineen – (alif-meem-noon). Amnun – Means peace, safety, a state of mind where one feels safe from fear or danger (2:24), safe, secure and at peace, peace of mind, to testify, the opposite of dishonesty To accept, to obey, to bow in obedience According to the Holy Quran, Eiman in the following five fundamental entities is demanded of one to become a Momin (2:177): Eiman in Allah means to have faith in His existence, to trust His every word, to depend upon the laws given by Him and declare that one would obey those laws. To have faith in the law of Mukafat means to

have firm conviction in that law and to have faith in the continuity of life after death. To have faith in Malaika means to believe that all heavenly forces operate in the universe to implement the tasks/programmes given to them by Allah, and that all heavenly forces have been made subservient to man. Eiman is usually translated in English as 'belief or 'faith', and 'faith in turn signifies blind acceptance without proof, argument, or reason. According to the Holy Quran, however, eiman is not what has been described as above as believing. In fact, eiman is synonymous with conviction and is based upon reason and knowledge. The Holy Quran does not recognize Eiman as any belief that is divorced from reason and involves the blind acceptance of any postulate. Eiman, according to the Holy Quran, signifies the conviction that results from full mental acceptance and intellectual satisfaction. This kind of conviction gives one a feeling of amn - inner contentment and peace (amn and Eiman have a common root)

11. Fitna – (fa-ta-noon) Fitna is used in the meaning of deviation or to go astray from the right path. In verse (22:11) it is used as opposite of khair (good). In verses (2:193, 8:39) it means to create chaos or disorder.

Overall, in the Quran it is used in the meaning of deviation in reference to the hurdles put in the way of establishing the Quranic social order.

12. Gabriel – Stands for the angel Jibraeel
13. Ghafoor – (ghain-fa-ra) It is one of the attributes of Allah. It means the One Who provides Maghfirah. Maghfirah means protection and also forgiveness. Maghfirah also means to save a person from the punishment that is the outcome of his misdeeds (Mobeei). Maghfirah is usually translated as forgiveness.
14. Hajj – (ha-jeem-jeem) The annual pilgrimage to Makkah.
15. Hamd – (ha-meem-dal) It is the expression of the deep, intense feeling of appreciation invoked spontaneously when one sees an exceptionally beautiful and unique thing. The intention of uttering hamd i.e. to say al-Hamdulillah) is to acknowledge the greatness of whoever created the given object of admiration. 'Hamd Bari-e-Taala' means to praise Allah.
16. Haqq – It is a very comprehensive Quranic term. It is usually translated in English as truth or right. No belief or theory relating to this world can be described as haqq

unless its truth is established by a positive manifestation of its.

17. Haram – (ha-ra-meem) Haram is antonym of halal, which means forbiddenand also a place whose protection is necessary. Ashbur-ul-harum is the four months (Rajab, Zequad, Zul-Hajj and Muharram) wherein all fights were forbidden (Taj/Moheet). The authority to prohibit certain things (declare them haram) rests with Allah alone (7:32–33, 2:172–173). No one else is authorised to exercise this right.
18. Hijra – (ha-jeem-ra) Albajro means to leave something, to move from, to remove it, to separate from. Therefore, alHijra or hijra means to leave one area and move to another - in other words, to emigrate.
19. Iblees – (ba-lam-seen) Ab-lasdmeati & to feel dejected (Tbn-e-Faris). It also means to get dazed and The Holy Quran has presented Iblees as an embodiment of rebellion, disobedience, insubordination and revolt. He refused to obey Allah, took up a rebellious path and became among those who disobey (2:24), as opposed to Malaika, whose nature is total obedience without doubt to Allah's command (38:73). The Quran has termed Iblees and Satan (SHAITAN) as the two faces of the same coin.

20. Injeel/the Gospel/the Bible – It is the name of the book revealed to Jesus.
21. Ishmael/Ismail – Ishmael was the elder of the two sons of Abraham, as mentioned in the Holy Quran.
22. Islam – (seen-lam-meem) This is the basic root for the most important words Islam and Muslim, necessitating, understanding its meaning fully and in depth. All the basic meanings have been taken from Lane, Taj. Islam means to bow in totality before the eternal laws given by Allah in letter and spirit. It is the only way of life which ensures reaching one's destiny (20:47) and anyone who follows a different path will be unable to bring about the expected results, and he ultimately will be doomed. Islam is that code of life, which has been revealed by Allah for mankind. There is no other code acceptable to Him. In Surah 3:82, the Quran says, "Do those people desire some different deen than the one ordained by Allah?" At yet another place, "If someone adopts a way other than this, it will not be acceptable and in the end he will be the loser (3:84)." This is the code, which was revealed to various anbiya from time to time. This final and complete code of life was revealed to Rasool - Allah ﷺ and selected the whole of mankind. This code

is called Al-Islam and the followers of the code are called Muslimeen (Muslims). A Muslim is he, who accepts the Holy Quran as the one and only complete and final code revealed by Allah for mankind.

23. Jacob/Yaqub/Yaqoob – Jacob was the son of Isaac, nephew of Ishma'el and grandson of Abraham. His title was Israel (man of Allah); that is why his generation is called the Bani-Israel the sons of Israel.
24. Jahannam – Generally, it means hell.
25. Jannah, Jannat – (jeem-noon-noon) It is usually translated as heaven or paradise.
26. Jesus – The name of Esa (Jesus) is mentioned 25 times and Maseeh, ibn-e-Maryam, 11 times in the Quran.
27. Kufr/kafir/kafireen – (kaf-f a-ra) Means to conceal, to hide, to cover. Keeping in view this meaning of hiding or covering, it was also used in the meaning of denial, refusal or rejection. Therefore, it was used in contrast to the concept of Eiman, i.e., one who denies the absolute truth as given in the Quran , In the Quran, the plural of kafir is given as kuffar, kafiroon or kafaratun. Then there are various categories of kafireen e.g, those who not only refuse to accept but also hinder others from accepting it, sometimes by force.

28. Mary/Maryam – The literal meaning of this word is highly placed. The Holy Quran mentions Mary as the mother of Jesus (Esa) (3:45).

29. Moses – Stands for the Messenger Musa.

30. Munafiqeen – (noon-fa-qaf) Munafiqeen (hypocrites): are those who in order to derive some benefits or personal gains join the Jamat-ul-momineen, but abandon them at the time of crisis after spreading , disheartening rumours.

31. Mushrikeen – See shirk.

32. Muslim – The Arabic word 'Muslim' is derived from three letters (Seen, Laam, Meem). These letters give the word its basic concept and characteristic meaning, salama - means purified, perfect, complete in all respects; free of blemish. aslarna the one who submits, bows (i) in totality before the eternal Divine Laws in letter and spirit; (ii) and leads a balanced life, A person who has the above traits is a Muslim. A body or a group of such people is called muslimeen, the followers of Islam. Hence, a Muslim is one who accepts the Holy Quran as the complete final Code of life revealed by the Sustainer of mankind.

33. Muttaqeen – (wao-qaf-ya) Muttaqee. a person who keeps away from things that are harmful to his personality and character, by adhering to the laws of Allah, thus rejecting a negative approach to life and accepting positive virtues and is conscious of his duties (See details under taqwa).

34. Firaun (Pharaoh) – It occurs in the Quran 74 times. The Pharaoh was the dynastic tide of Egyptian kings who ruled Egypt and were called Firaun.

35. Rabb, Rabubiyya – (ra-ba-ba) It is usually translated into English as the Lord, which does not convey the real meanings and significance of the Arabic word. It means one who provides nourishment, to process a thing with new additions, alterations or changes so that it should reach its Rabb means Nourisher, Cherisher and Sustaniner.

36. Shiateen – (plural of Shaitan).

37. Taqwa – (wao-qaf-ya) The common English equivalent, namely, piety, does not properly express the real meaning of the word. Taqwa would mean to obey and follow the laws of Allah. Surah Muhammad explains that there are some people who follow their own ambitions, feelings or desires and others, who follow the laws of Allah the

later category gets or attains taqwa (47:1 7) Therefore, muttaqeen are those people who keep away from things that are harmful to their personalities, by remaining in harmony with the laws of Allah, and thus get their personalities developed. Asad has used the term 'Allah-conscious' for Taqwa.

38. Wahi – (wao-ha-ya) - (Divine revelation) 'Wahi'is the Quranic term for divine message from Allah to His Messengers.
39. Zikr – (za-kaf-ra) To discuss, relate or mention The Divine laws are also called Zikrullah (39:23).

WHAT THE QURAN SAYS ABOUT ITSELF

This (Quran) is the Book; in it is guidance sure, without doubt, to those who fear Allah.

2:2

ذٰلِكَ الْكِتٰبُ لَا رَيْبَ ۛۚ فِيْهِ ۛۚ هُدًى لِّلْمُتَّقِيْنَ ۙ﴿۲﴾

And if you doubt any part of what
We have revealed from on high,
step by step, upon Our servant
(Muhammad), then produce a Surah
of similar merit, and call upon any
other than Allah to bear witness for
you-if what you say is true!

2:23

وَاِنْ كُنْتُمْ فِيْ رَيْبٍ مِّمَّا نَزَّلْنَا عَلٰى
عَبْدِنَا فَاْتُوْا بِسُوْرَةٍ مِّنْ مِّثْلِهٖ ۠
وَادْعُوْا شُهَدَآءَكُمْ مِّنْ دُوْنِ اللّٰهِ اِنْ
كُنْتُمْ صٰدِقِيْنَ ﴿٢٣﴾

And believe in what I reveal,
confirming the revelation which
is with you, and be not the first to
reject Faith therein, nor sell My Signs
for a small price; and fear Me, and
Me alone.

2:41

وَاٰمِنُوْا بِمَآ اَنْزَلْتُ مُصَدِّقًا لِّمَا
مَعَكُمْ وَلَا تَكُوْنُوْٓا اَوَّلَ كَافِرٍۭ بِهٖ ۠
وَلَا تَشْتَرُوْا بِاٰيٰتِيْ ثَمَنًا قَلِيْلًا ز وَّ
اِيَّايَ فَاتَّقُوْنِ ﴿٤١﴾

Miserable is the price for which they have sold their souls, in that they deny (the Revelation) which Allah sent down, in insolent envy that Allah of His Grace should send it to any of His servants He pleases: Thus have they drawn on themselves Wrath upon Wrath. And humiliating is the punishment for those who reject Faith.

2:90

بِئْسَمَا اشْتَرَوْا بِهٖٓ اَنْفُسَهُمْ اَنْ
يَّكْفُرُوْا بِمَآ اَنْزَلَ اللّٰهُ بَغْيًا اَنْ
يُّنَزِّلَ اللّٰهُ مِنْ فَضْلِهٖ عَلٰى مَنْ يَّشَآءُ
مِنْ عِبَادِهٖ ۚ فَبَآءُوْ بِغَضَبٍ عَلٰى
غَضَبٍ ۗ وَلِلْكٰفِرِيْنَ عَذَابٌ
مُّهِيْنٌ ﴿٩٠﴾

When it is said to them, "Believe in what Allah has revealed (Quran)," they say, "We believe in what was sent down to us:" yet they reject all besides, even if it be Truth confirming what is with them. Say (O Muhammad): "Why then have you slain the messengers of Allah in times gone by, if you did indeed believe?"

2:91

وَاِذَا قِيْلَ لَهُمْ اٰمِنُوْا بِمَآ اَنْزَلَ
اللّٰهُ قَالُوْا نُؤْمِنُ بِمَآ اُنْزِلَ عَلَيْنَا
وَيَكْفُرُوْنَ بِمَا وَرَآءَهٗ ق وَهُوَ الْحَقُّ
مُصَدِّقًا لِّمَا مَعَهُمْ ط قُلْ فَلِمَ تَقْتُلُوْنَ
اَنْۢبِيَآءَ اللّٰهِ مِنْ قَبْلُ اِنْ كُنْتُمْ
مُّؤْمِنِيْنَ ﴿٩١﴾

Those who conceal the clear (Signs) We have revealed, and the Guidance, after We have made it clear for the people in the Book,- on them shall be Allah's curse, and the curse of those entitled to curse,- Except those who repent and make amends and openly declare (the Truth): To them I turn; for I am Oft-returning, Most Merciful.

2:159, 160

اِنَّ الَّذِيْنَ يَكْتُمُوْنَ مَآ اَنْزَلْنَا
مِنَ الْبَيِّنٰتِ وَالْهُدٰى مِنْۢ بَعْدِ مَا
بَيَّنّٰهُ لِلنَّاسِ فِى الْكِتٰبِۙ اُولٰٓئِكَ
يَلْعَنُهُمُ اللّٰهُ وَيَلْعَنُهُمُ اللّٰعِنُوْنَۙ ﴿١٥٩﴾
اِلَّا الَّذِيْنَ تَابُوْا وَاَصْلَحُوْا وَبَيَّنُوْا
فَاُولٰٓئِكَ اَتُوْبُ عَلَيْهِمْۚ وَاَنَا
التَّوَّابُ الرَّحِيْمُ ﴿١٦٠﴾

Thus it is: since it is Allah who bestows the divine writ (Quran) from on high, setting forth the truth, all those who set their own views against the divine writ (Quran) are, surely, most deeply in the wrong.

2:176

ذٰلِكَ بِاَنَّ اللّٰهَ نَزَّلَ الۡكِتٰبَ بِالۡحَقِّ ؕ وَ
اِنَّ الَّذِيۡنَ اخۡتَلَفُوۡا فِى الۡكِتٰبِ لَفِىۡ
شِقَاقٍۭ بَعِيۡدٍ ﴿۱۷۶﴾ ع

Ramadhan
is the (month) in
which was sent down
the Quran, as a Guide to
mankind, also clear (Signs)
for Guidance and Judgment
(Between right and wrong). So
every one of you who is present (at
his home) during that month should
spend it in fasting, but if any one
is ill, or on a journey, the prescribed
period (Should be made up) by days
later. Allah intends every facility for
you; He does not want to put you
to difficulties. (He wants you) to
complete the prescribed period (of
Ramadan), and to glorify Him in
that He has Guided you; and
so that you may be grateful
to Him.

2:185

شَهْرُ
رَمَضَانَ الَّذِیْۤ
اُنْزِلَ فِیْهِ الْقُرْاٰنُ هُدًى
لِّلنَّاسِ وَبَیِّنٰتٍ مِّنَ الْهُدٰى
وَالْفُرْقَانِ ۚ فَمَنْ شَهِدَ مِنْكُمُ
الشَّهْرَ فَلْیَصُمْهُ ؕ وَمَنْ كَانَ
مَرِیْضًا اَوْ عَلٰى سَفَرٍ فَعِدَّةٌ مِّنْ اَیَّامٍ
اُخَرَ ؕ یُرِیْدُ اللّٰهُ بِكُمُ الْیُسْرَ وَلَا
یُرِیْدُ بِكُمُ الْعُسْرَ ٘ وَلِتُكْمِلُوا
الْعِدَّةَ وَلِتُكَبِّرُوا اللّٰهَ عَلٰى
مَا هَدٰىكُمْ وَلَعَلَّكُمْ
تَشْكُرُوْنَ ﴿۱۸۵﴾

All mankind
were once one single
community; (then they
began to differ) whereupon
Allah raised up the Messengers
as heralds of glad tidings and as
warner, and through them bestowed
Revelation from on high, setting
forth the truth, so that it might decide
between people with regard to all on
which they had come to hold divergent
views. Yet none other than the same people
who had been granted this (Revelation)
began, out of mutual jealousy, to disagree
about its meaning after all evidence of
the truth had come unto them. But
Allah guided the believers to the truth
about which, by His leave, they had
disagreed: for Allah guides onto a
straight way him that wills (to
be guided)

2:213

كَانَ النَّاسُ اُمَّةً
وَّاحِدَةً قف فَبَعَثَ اللّٰهُ
النَّبِيّٖنَ مُبَشِّرِيْنَ وَمُنْذِرِيْنَ ص
وَاَنْزَلَ مَعَهُمُ الْكِتٰبَ بِالْحَقِّ
لِيَحْكُمَ بَيْنَ النَّاسِ فِيْمَا اخْتَلَفُوْا
فِيْهِ ط وَمَا اخْتَلَفَ فِيْهِ اِلَّا الَّذِيْنَ
اُوْتُوْهُ مِنْۢ بَعْدِ مَا جَآءَتْهُمُ الْبَيِّنٰتُ
بَغْيًاۢ بَيْنَهُمْ ج فَهَدَى اللّٰهُ الَّذِيْنَ اٰمَنُوْا
لِمَا اخْتَلَفُوْا فِيْهِ مِنَ الْحَقِّ بِاِذْنِهٖ ط
وَاللّٰهُ يَهْدِيْ مَنْ يَّشَآءُ اِلٰى
صِرٰطٍ مُّسْتَقِيْمٍ ﴿٢١٣﴾

And so, when
you divorce women
and they are about
to reach the end of their
waiting-term, then either
retain them in a fair manner or
let them go in a fair manner. But
do not retain them against their will
in order to hurt (them): for he who
does so sins indeed against himself.
And do not take (these) messages of
God in a frivolous spirit; and remember
the blessings with which God has
graced you, and all the revelation and
the wisdom which He has bestowed
on you from on high in order
to admonish you thereby; and
remain conscious of Allah, and
know that Allah has full
knowledge of everything.

2:231

وَ اِذَا طَلَّقْتُمُ

النِّسَآءَ فَبَلَغْنَ

اَجَلَهُنَّ فَاَمْسِكُوْهُنَّ

بِمَعْرُوْفٍ اَوْ سَرِّحُوْهُنَّ

بِمَعْرُوْفٍ ۠ وَّ لَا تُمْسِكُوْهُنَّ ضِرَارًا

لِّتَعْتَدُوْا ۚ وَمَنْ يَّفْعَلْ ذٰلِكَ فَقَدْ ظَلَمَ

نَفْسَهٗ ؕ وَلَا تَتَّخِذُوْٓا اٰيٰتِ اللّٰهِ هُزُوًا ۫ وَ

اذْكُرُوْا نِعْمَتَ اللّٰهِ عَلَيْكُمْ وَمَآ اَنْزَلَ

عَلَيْكُمْ مِّنَ الْكِتٰبِ وَالْحِكْمَةِ

يَعِظُكُمْ بِهٖ ؕ وَاتَّقُوا اللّٰهَ

وَاعْلَمُوْٓا اَنَّ اللّٰهَ بِكُلِّ شَيْءٍ

عَلِيْمٌ ﴿٢٣١﴾ ع

Step by step has He bestowed upon thee from on high this Divine book, setting forth the truth which confirms whatever there still remains (of earlier Revelations): for it is He Who has bestowed from on high the Torah and the Gospel (Injeel).

3:3

نَزَّلَ عَلَيْكَ الْكِتٰبَ بِالْحَقِّ مُصَدِّقًا
لِّمَا بَيْنَ يَدَيْهِ وَاَنْزَلَ التَّوْرٰىةَ
وَالْاِنْجِيْلَ ﴿٣﴾ۙ

He it
is Who has
bestowed upon thee
from on high this Quran,
containing messages that
are clear in and by themselves
- and these are the essence of the
Quran - as well as others that are
allegorical. Now those whose hearts
are given to swerving from the truth go
after that part of the Quran which has
been expressed in allegory, seeking out
(what is bound to create) confusion, and
seeking (to arrive at) its final meaning
(in an arbitrary manner); but none
save Allah knows its final meaning.
Hence, those who are deeply rooted
in knowledge say: "We believe in it;
the whole (of the Quran) is from
our Sustainer – only those
take this to heart who are
endowed with insight."

3:7

هُوَ الَّذِیۡۤ
اَنۡزَلَ عَلَیۡكَ
الۡكِتٰبَ مِنۡهُ اٰیٰتٌ
مُّحۡكَمٰتٌ هُنَّ اُمُّ الۡكِتٰبِ
وَاُخَرُ مُتَشٰبِهٰتٌ ؕ فَاَمَّا الَّذِیۡنَ فِیۡ
قُلُوۡبِهِمۡ زَیۡغٌ فَیَتَّبِعُوۡنَ مَا تَشٰبَهَ مِنۡهُ
ابۡتِغَآءَ الۡفِتۡنَةِ وَابۡتِغَآءَ تَاۡوِیۡلِهٖ ؔۚ
وَمَا یَعۡلَمُ تَاۡوِیۡلَهٗۤ اِلَّا اللّٰهُ ؔؕ
وَالرّٰسِخُوۡنَ فِی الۡعِلۡمِ یَقُوۡلُوۡنَ
اٰمَنَّا بِهٖ ۙ كُلٌّ مِّنۡ عِنۡدِ رَبِّنَا ۚ
وَمَا یَذَّكَّرُ اِلَّاۤ اُولُوا
الۡاَلۡبٰبِ ﴿۷﴾

O you People of the Book!
Believe in what We have (now)
revealed, confirming what was
(already) with you, before there is
a confrontation in which they will
suffer a crushing defeat and be defaced
beyond recognition being cast away
from Allah as the Sabbath-breakers
were, for the decision of Allah must
be carried out.

4:47

يٰۤاَيُّهَا الَّذِيْنَ اُوْتُوا الْكِتٰبَ
اٰمِنُوْا بِمَا نَزَّلْنَا مُصَدِّقًا لِّمَا
مَعَكُمْ مِّنْ قَبْلِ اَنْ نَّطْمِسَ وُجُوْهًا
فَنَرُدَّهَا عَلٰۤى اَدْبَارِهَاۤ اَوْ نَلْعَنَهُمْ
كَمَا لَعَنَّاۤ اَصْحٰبَ السَّبْتِ ؕ وَكَانَ
اَمْرُ اللّٰهِ مَفْعُوْلًا ﴿۴۷﴾

Do they not consider the Quran (with care)? Had it been from other than Allah, they would surely have found therein much discrepancy.

4:82

اَفَلَا يَتَدَبَّرُوْنَ الْقُرْاٰنَ ؕ وَلَوْ كَانَ
مِنْ عِنْدِ غَيْرِ اللّٰهِ لَوَجَدُوْا فِيْهِ
اخْتِلَافًا كَثِيْرًا ﴿۸۲﴾

We have sent down to you the
Book in truth, that you might judge
between men, as guided by Allah, so
do not be (used) as an advocate by
those who betray trust.

4:105

إِنَّآ اَنْزَلْنَآ اِلَيْكَ الْكِتٰبَ بِالْحَقِّ

لِتَحْكُمَ بَيْنَ النَّاسِ بِمَآ اَرٰىكَ اللّٰهُ ط

وَلَا تَكُنْ لِّلْخَآئِنِيْنَ خَصِيْمًا ﴿١٠٥﴾ لا

And but for Allah's favour upon you and His grace, some of those (who are false to themselves) would indeed endeavour to lead you astray; yet none but themselves do they lead astray. Nor can they harm you in any way, since Allah has revealed upon you from on high this Divine book (Quran and (given thee) wisdom, and has imparted to you the knowledge of what you did not know. And Allah's favour upon you is tremendous indeed.

4:113

وَلَوْلَا فَضْلُ اللّٰهِ عَلَيْكَ
وَرَحْمَتُهٗ لَهَمَّتْ طَّآىِٕفَةٌ مِّنْهُمْ اَنْ
يُّضِلُّوْكَ ؕ وَمَا يُضِلُّوْنَ اِلَّآ اَنْفُسَهُمْ
وَمَا يَضُرُّوْنَكَ مِنْ شَيْءٍ ؕ وَاَنْزَلَ اللّٰهُ
عَلَيْكَ الْكِتٰبَ وَالْحِكْمَةَ وَعَلَّمَكَ
مَا لَمْ تَكُنْ تَعْلَمُ ؕ وَكَانَ فَضْلُ اللّٰهِ
عَلَيْكَ عَظِيْمًا ﴿۱۱۳﴾

O you who believe! Believe in Allah and His Messenger, and the scripture (Quran) which He has sent to His Messenger and the scriptures which He sent to those before (him). Anyone who denies Allah, His Angels, His Books, His Messenger., and the Day of Judgment, has gone far, far astray.

4:136

يٰٓاَيُّهَا الَّذِيْنَ اٰمَنُوْٓا اٰمِنُوْا بِاللّٰهِ
وَرَسُوْلِهٖ وَالْكِتٰبِ الَّذِيْ نَزَّلَ عَلٰى
رَسُوْلِهٖ وَالْكِتٰبِ الَّذِيْٓ اَنْزَلَ مِنْ
قَبْلُ ؕ وَمَنْ يَّكْفُرْ بِاللّٰهِ وَمَلٰٓئِكَتِهٖ
وَكُتُبِهٖ وَرُسُلِهٖ وَالْيَوْمِ الْاٰخِرِ
فَقَدْ ضَلَّ ضَلٰلًاۢ بَعِيْدًا ﴿١٣٦﴾

But those among them who are well-grounded in knowledge, and the believers, believe in what has been revealed to you and what was revealed before you: And (especially) those who establish regular prayer and practise regular charity and believe in Allah and in the Last Day: To them shall We soon give a great reward.

4:162

لٰكِنِ الرّٰسِخُوْنَ فِى الْعِلْمِ
مِنْهُمْ وَالْمُؤْمِنُوْنَ يُؤْمِنُوْنَ بِمَآ
اُنْزِلَ اِلَيْكَ وَمَآ اُنْزِلَ مِنْ قَبْلِكَ
وَالْمُقِيْمِيْنَ الصَّلٰوةَ وَالْمُؤْتُوْنَ
الزَّكٰوةَ وَالْمُؤْمِنُوْنَ بِاللّٰهِ وَالْيَوْمِ
الْاٰخِرِ ؕ اُولٰٓئِكَ سَنُؤْتِيْهِمْ اَجْرًا
عَظِيْمًا ﴿١٦٢﴾ ع

And to you (O
Messenger) have We
vouchsafed this (Quran) ,
setting forth the truth, confirming
the truth of whatever there still
remains of earlier revelations and
determining what is true therein. Judge,
then, between the followers of earlier
revelations in accordance with what Allah
has bestowed from on high, and do not
follow their errant views, forsaking the truth
that has come unto thee. Unto every one of
you have We appointed a (different) law and
way of life. And if Allah had so willed, He
could surely have made you all one single
community: but (He willed it otherwise)
in order to test you by means of what He
has vouchsafed unto, you. Compete, then,
with one another in doing good works !
To Allah you all must return; and then
He will make you truly understand
all that on which you differed.

5:48

وَ اَنۡزَلۡنَاۤ اِلَیۡکَ

الۡکِتٰبَ بِالۡحَقِّ مُصَدِّقًا

لِّمَا بَیۡنَ یَدَیۡہِ مِنَ الۡکِتٰبِ

وَ مُہَیۡمِنًا عَلَیۡہِ فَاحۡکُمۡ بَیۡنَہُمۡ

بِمَاۤ اَنۡزَلَ اللّٰہُ وَ لَا تَتَّبِعۡ اَہۡوَآءَہُمۡ عَمَّا

جَآءَکَ مِنَ الۡحَقِّ ؕ لِکُلٍّ جَعَلۡنَا مِنۡکُمۡ

شِرۡعَۃً وَّ مِنۡہَاجًا ؕ وَ لَوۡ شَآءَ اللّٰہُ لَجَعَلَکُمۡ

اُمَّۃً وَّاحِدَۃً وَّ لٰکِنۡ لِّیَبۡلُوَکُمۡ فِیۡ مَاۤ

اٰتٰىکُمۡ فَاسۡتَبِقُوا الۡخَیۡرٰتِ ؕ اِلَی اللّٰہِ

مَرۡجِعُکُمۡ جَمِیۡعًا فَیُنَبِّئُکُمۡ بِمَا

کُنۡتُمۡ فِیۡہِ تَخۡتَلِفُوۡنَ ﴿ۙ۴۸﴾

For, certainly, those who have attained to faith (in this Quran), as well as those who follow the Jewish faith, and the Sabians, and the Christians–all who believe in Allah and the Last Day and do righteous deeds–no fear need they have, and neither shall they grieve.

5:69

اِنَّ الَّذِيْنَ اٰمَنُوْا وَالَّذِيْنَ هَادُوْا
وَالصّٰبِـُٔوْنَ وَالنَّصٰرٰى مَنْ اٰمَنَ بِاللّٰهِ
وَالْيَوْمِ الْاٰخِرِ وَعَمِلَ صٰلِحًا فَلَا
خَوْفٌ عَلَيْهِمْ وَلَا هُمْ يَحْزَنُوْنَ ﴿٦٩﴾

Had they believed in Allah and His Messenger and what was revealed to him (Quran), they would not have taken those who deny the truth as their friends and protectors, but most of them are rebellious wrong-doers.

5:81

وَلَوْ كَانُوْا يُؤْمِنُوْنَ بِاللّٰهِ وَالنَّبِيِّ
وَمَآ اُنْزِلَ اِلَيْهِ مَا اتَّخَذُوْهُمْ اَوْلِيَآءَ
وَلٰكِنَّ كَثِيْرًا مِّنْهُمْ فٰسِقُوْنَ ﴿٨١﴾

O you who have attained to faith! Do not ask about matters which, if they were to be made manifest to you (in terms of law), might cause you hardship; for, if you should ask about them while the Quran is being revealed, they might (indeed) be made manifest to you (as laws). Allah has absolved (you from any obligation) in this respect: for Allah is much-Forgiving, Forbearing.

5:101

يٰٓاَيُّهَا الَّذِيْنَ اٰمَنُوْا لَا تَسْـَٔلُوْا عَنْ
اَشْيَآءَ اِنْ تُبْدَ لَكُمْ تَسُؤْكُمْ ۚ وَ
اِنْ تَسْـَٔلُوْا عَنْهَا حِيْنَ يُنَزَّلُ الْقُرْاٰنُ
تُبْدَ لَكُمْ ؕ عَفَا اللّٰهُ عَنْهَا ؕ وَاللّٰهُ
غَفُوْرٌ حَلِيْمٌ ﴿١٠١﴾

Say: What thing is most weighty in evidence? Say: (Allah) is witness between me and you; This Qur›an hath been revealed to me by inspiration, that I may warn you and all whom it reaches. Can ye possibly bear witness that besides Allah there is another Allah." Say: "Nay! I cannot bear witness!" Say: "But in truth He is the one Allah, and I truly am innocent of (your blasphemy of) joining others with Him."

6:19

قُلْ اَیُّ شَیْءٍ اَکْبَرُ شَهٰدَةً ؕ قُلِ
اللّٰهُ ۙ قف شَهِیْدٌۢ بَیْنِیْ وَ بَیْنَکُمْ ۙ قف
وَ اُوْحِیَ اِلَیَّ هٰذَا الْقُرْاٰنُ لِاُنْذِرَکُمْ
بِهٖ وَمَنْۢ بَلَغَ ؕ اَئِنَّکُمْ لَتَشْهَدُوْنَ اَنَّ
مَعَ اللّٰهِ اٰلِهَةً اُخْرٰی ؕ قُلْ لَّاۤ اَشْهَدُ ۚ
قُلْ اِنَّمَا هُوَ اِلٰهٌ وَّاحِدٌ وَّ اِنَّنِیْ
بَرِیْٓءٌ مِّمَّا تُشْرِکُوْنَ ﴿۱۹﴾

And this, too, is a Divine
book (Quran) which We have
bestowed from on high-blessed,
confirming the truth of whatever
there still remains (of earlier
revelations) -and (this) in order that
you may warn the foremost of all cities
(Makkah) and all who dwell around
it. And those who believe in the life
to come do believe in this (warning);
and it is they who are ever-mindful
of their prayers.

6:92

وَ هٰذَا كِتٰبٌ اَنْزَلْنٰهُ مُبٰرَكٌ
مُّصَدِّقُ الَّذِىْ بَيْنَ يَدَيْهِ وَ لِتُنْذِرَ
اُمَّ الْقُرٰى وَ مَنْ حَوْلَهَا ؕ وَالَّذِيْنَ
يُؤْمِنُوْنَ بِالْاٰخِرَةِ يُؤْمِنُوْنَ بِهٖ وَ
هُمْ عَلٰى صَلَاتِهِمْ يُحَافِظُوْنَ ﴿٩٢﴾

Means of insight have now come to you from your Sustainer (through the Quran). Whoever, therefore, chooses to see, does so for his own good; and whoever chooses to remain blind, does so to his own hurt. And (say unto the blind of heart): "I am not your keeper."

6:104

قَدْ جَآءَكُمْ بَصَآئِرُ مِنْ رَّبِّكُمْ ۚ فَمَنْ
اَبْصَرَ فَلِنَفْسِهٖ ۚ وَمَنْ عَمِيَ فَعَلَيْهَا ؕ
وَمَآ اَنَا عَلَيْكُمْ بِحَفِيْظٍ ﴿١٠٤﴾

(say thou:) Am I, then, to
look unto anyone but Allah
for judgment(as to what is right
and wrong), when it is He who has
bestowed upon you from on high this
divine writ, clearly spelling out the
truth?"And those unto whom We have
vouchsafed revelation afore-time know
that this one, too, has been bestowed
from on high, step by step, by thy
Sustainer. Be not, then, among
the doubters.

6:114

اَفَغَيْرَ اللّٰهِ اَبْتَغِيْ حَكَمًا وَّهُوَ
الَّذِيْٓ اَنْزَلَ اِلَيْكُمُ الْكِتٰبَ
مُفَصَّلًا ؕ وَالَّذِيْنَ اٰتَيْنٰهُمُ الْكِتٰبَ
يَعْلَمُوْنَ اَنَّهٗ مُنَزَّلٌ مِّنْ رَّبِّكَ بِالْحَقِّ
فَلَا تَكُوْنَنَّ مِنَ الْمُمْتَرِيْنَ ١١٤

And this, too, is a Divine Book which We have bestowed from on high, a blessed one: follow it, then, and be conscious of Allah, so that you might be graced with His mercy.

6:155

وَهٰذَا كِتٰبٌ اَنْزَلْنٰهُ مُبٰرَكٌ فَاتَّبِعُوْهُ
وَاتَّقُوْا لَعَلَّكُمْ تُرْحَمُوْنَ ﴿١٥٥﴾ لا

(It has been given to you) lest you say, “Only unto two groups of people, (both of them) before our time, has a divine writ been bestowed from on highand we were indeed unaware of their teachings.

6:156

اَنْ تَقُوْلُوْٓا اِنَّمَآ اُنْزِلَ الْكِتٰبُ عَلٰى
طَآىِٕفَتَيْنِ مِنْ قَبْلِنَا ۖ وَاِنْ كُنَّا عَنْ
دِرَاسَتِهِمْ لَغٰفِلِيْنَ ﴿١٥٦﴾ لا

This Book has
been sent down to
you so that you may not
say, "If a Divine Book had
been bestowed from on high
upon us, we would surely have
followed its guidance better than
they (Jews and Christians) did."
And so, a clear evidence of the truth
has now come unto you from your
Sustainer, and Guidance, and Grace.
Who, then, could be more wicked
than he who gives the lie to Allah's
messages, and turns away from
them in disdain? We shall repay
those who turn away from Our
messages in disdain with evil
suffering for having thus
turned away!

6:157

اَوْ تَقُوْلُوْا لَوْ اَنَّاۤ اُنْزِلَ
عَلَيْنَا الْكِتٰبُ لَكُنَّاۤ اَهْدٰى
مِنْهُمْ ۚ فَقَدْ جَآءَكُمْ بَيِّنَةٌ مِّنْ
رَّبِّكُمْ وَهُدًى وَّرَحْمَةٌ ۚ فَمَنْ
اَظْلَمُ مِمَّنْ كَذَّبَ بِاٰيٰتِ اللّٰهِ وَصَدَفَ
عَنْهَا ؕ سَنَجْزِى الَّذِيْنَ يَصْدِفُوْنَ
عَنْ اٰيٰتِنَا سُوْٓءَ الْعَذَابِ بِمَا
كَانُوْا يَصْدِفُوْنَ ﴿١٥٧﴾

A Divine Writ (Quran) has been bestowed from on high upon thee and let there be no doubt about this in thy heart-in order that you may warn (the erring) thereby, and (thus) admonish the believers.

7:2

كِتَٰبٌ أُنزِلَ إِلَيْكَ فَلَا يَكُن فِي
صَدْرِكَ حَرَجٌ مِّنْهُ لِتُنذِرَ بِهِۦ وَ
ذِكْرَىٰ لِلْمُؤْمِنِينَ ٢

Follow (O men!) the Revelation given to you from your Sustainer (Rabb), and follow not, as friends or protectors, other than Him. Little it is you remember of admonition.

7:3

اِتَّبِعُوْا مَآ اُنْزِلَ اِلَيْكُمْ مِّنْ رَّبِّكُمْ وَ
لَا تَتَّبِعُوْا مِنْ دُوْنِهٖٓ اَوْلِيَآءَ ؕ قَلِيْلًا
مَّا تَذَكَّرُوْنَ ۝۳

When you (Muhammad) do not bring them a sign, they say, "Why do you not invent one ?" Say: "I but follow what is revealed to me from my Sustainer (Rabb): This book (Quran) is an enlightenment from your Sustainer (Rabb) and a Guide and Mercy to the believers."

7:203

وَ اِذَا لَمْ تَاْتِهِمْ بِاٰيَةٍ قَالُوْا لَوْلَا
اجْتَبَيْتَهَا ؕ قُلْ اِنَّمَآ اَتَّبِعُ مَا
يُوْحٰٓى اِلَيَّ مِنْ رَّبِّيْ ۚ هٰذَا بَصَآئِرُ
مِنْ رَّبِّكُمْ وَهُدًى وَّرَحْمَةٌ لِّقَوْمٍ
يُّؤْمِنُوْنَ ﴿٢٠٣﴾

And yet, when you (O Prophet) do not produce any miracle for them, some (people) say, "Why do you not seek to obtain it (from Allah)? Say: "I only follow whatever is being revealed to me by my Sustainer: this (Revelation) is a means of insight from your Sustainer, and a Guidance and Grace to people who will believe.

7:203

وَ اِذَا لَمْ تَاْتِهِمْ بِاٰيَةٍ قَالُوْا لَوْلَا
اجْتَبَيْتَهَا ؕ قُلْ اِنَّمَآ اَتَّبِعُ مَا
يُوْحٰٓى اِلَىَّ مِنْ رَّبِّىْ ۚ هٰذَا بَصَآئِرُ
مِنْ رَّبِّكُمْ وَهُدًى وَّرَحْمَةٌ لِّقَوْمٍ
يُّؤْمِنُوْنَ ﴿٢٠٣﴾

Behold, Allah has bought
of the believers their lives and
their possessions, promising
them paradise in return, (and
so) they fight in Allah's cause,
and slay, and are slain: a promise
which in truth He has willed upon
Himself in (the words of) the Torah,
and the Gospel, and the Quran. And
who could be more faithful to his
covenant than Allah? Rejoice, then,
in the bargain which you have made
with Him: for this, this is the
triumph supreme!

9:111

اِنَّ اللّٰهَ اشْتَرٰی مِنَ
الْمُؤْمِنِيْنَ اَنْفُسَهُمْ وَ
اَمْوٰلَهُمْ بِاَنَّ لَهُمُ الْجَنَّةَ ؕ
يُقٰتِلُوْنَ فِيْ سَبِيْلِ اللّٰهِ فَيَقْتُلُوْنَ
وَ يُقْتَلُوْنَ ۫ وَعْدًا عَلَيْهِ حَقًّا فِي
التَّوْرٰىةِ وَ الْاِنْجِيْلِ وَ الْقُرْاٰنِ ؕ وَمَنْ
اَوْفٰى بِعَهْدِهٖ مِنَ اللّٰهِ فَاسْتَبْشِرُوْا
بِبَيْعِكُمُ الَّذِيْ بَايَعْتُمْ بِهٖ ؕ وَ
ذٰلِكَ هُوَ الْفَوْزُ الْعَظِيْمُ ﴿١١١﴾

Alif Lam. Ra. These are Messeges of the Divine Writ (Quran), full of wisdom.

10:1

الٓرٰ قف تِلْكَ اٰيٰتُ الْكِتٰبِ الْحَكِيْمِ ﴿١﴾

And (thus it is:) whenever
Our messages are conveyed
unto them in all their clarity,
those who do not believe that
they are destined to meet Us (are
wont to) say, Bring us a discourse
other than this, or alter this one."Say
(O Messenger): "It is not conceivable
that I should change it of my own
will; I only follow what is revealed to
me. Behold, I would dread, were I
(thus) to rebel against my Sustainer
(Rabb), the suffering (which would
befall me) on that , awesome Day
(of Judgment)!"

10:15

وَ اِذَا تُتْلٰى عَلَيْهِمْ اٰيَاتُنَا بَيِّنٰتٍ

قَالَ الَّذِيْنَ لَا يَرْجُوْنَ لِقَآءَنَا ۙ

ائْتِ بِقُرْاٰنٍ غَيْرِ هٰذَآ اَوْ بَدِّلْهُ ؕ

قُلْ مَا يَكُوْنُ لِيْٓ اَنْ اُبَدِّلَهٗ مِنْ تِلْقَآئِ

نَفْسِيْ ۚ اِنْ اَتَّبِعُ اِلَّا مَا يُوْحٰٓى اِلَيَّ ۚ

اِنِّيْٓ اَخَافُ اِنْ عَصَيْتُ رَبِّيْ عَذَابَ

يَوْمٍ عَظِيْمٍ ﴿١٥﴾

Say: Had Allah willed it (otherwise), I would not have conveyed this (Quran) unto you, nor would He have brought it to your knowledge. Indeed. a whole lifetime have I dwelt among you before this (revelation came unto me): will you not, then, use your reason?"

10:16

قُلْ لَّوْ شَآءَ اللّٰهُ مَا تَلَوْتُهٗ عَلَيْكُمْ
وَلَآ اَدْرٰىكُمْ بِهٖ ۖ فَقَدْ لَبِثْتُ فِيْكُمْ
عُمُرًا مِّنْ قَبْلِهٖ ۗ اَفَلَا تَعْقِلُوْنَ ﴿١٦﴾

And this Quran is not such as could ever be invented despite of Allah; but it is a confirmation of that which was before it and an exposition of that which is decreed for mankind-- There is nothing doubtful in this Book which is from the Sustainer of the Worlds.

10:37

وَمَا كَانَ هٰذَا الْقُرْاٰنُ اَنْ يُّفْتَرٰى مِنْ
دُوْنِ اللّٰهِ وَلٰكِنْ تَصْدِيْقَ الَّذِىْ بَيْنَ
يَدَيْهِ وَتَفْصِيْلَ الْكِتٰبِ لَا رَيْبَ فِيْهِ
مِنْ رَّبِّ الْعٰلَمِيْنَ ﴿٣٧﴾ قف

O mankind! There has now come unto you an admonition (warning) from your Sustainer (Rabb), and a cure for all (the ill) that may be in men's hearts, and Guidance and Grace to all who believe (in Him).

10:57

يٰٓاَيُّهَا النَّاسُ قَدْ جَآءَتْكُمْ مَّوْعِظَةٌ
مِّنْ رَّبِّكُمْ وَشِفَآءٌ لِّمَا فِى الصُّدُوْرِ ۙ۵ لا
وَهُدًى وَّرَحْمَةٌ لِّلْمُؤْمِنِيْنَ ﴿۵۷﴾

And in whatever condition
you may find yourself, (O
Messenger,) and whatever
discourse of this (divine writ)
you may be reciting, and whatever
work you (all, O men,) may do
-(remember that) We are your
witness(from the moment) when you
enter upon it: for, not even an atom's
weight (of whatever there is) on earth
or in heaven escapes thy Sustainer's
(Rabb) knowledge; and neither is
there anything smaller than that,
or larger, but is recorded in (His)
clear decree.

10:61

وَمَا تَكُوْنُ فِيْ شَاْنٍ وَّمَا
تَتْلُوْا مِنْهُ مِنْ قُرْاٰنٍ وَّلَا
تَعْمَلُوْنَ مِنْ عَمَلٍ اِلَّا كُنَّا
عَلَيْكُمْ شُهُوْدًا اِذْ تُفِيْضُوْنَ فِيْهِ ط
وَمَا يَعْزُبُ عَنْ رَّبِّكَ مِنْ مِّثْقَالِ ذَرَّةٍ
فِي الْاَرْضِ وَلَا فِي السَّمَآءِ وَلَآ اَصْغَرَ
مِنْ ذٰلِكَ وَلَآ اَكْبَرَ اِلَّا فِيْ كِتٰبٍ
مُّبِيْنٍ ﴿٦١﴾

Alif. Lam. Ra. (This is) a Book whose foundations rest upon strong foundations and have been revealed clearly by One Who is all-Wise and all-Informed: Serve none but Allah. Say to them (Muhammad) 'I have come to you to warn you about the consequences of wrong doings and to give you glad tidings about the results of good deeds'.

11:1

الٓرٰ ۟ قف كِتٰبٌ اُحۡكِمَتۡ اٰيٰتُهٗ ثُمَّ

فُصِّلَتۡ مِنۡ لَّدُنۡ حَكِيۡمٍ خَبِيۡرٍ ۙ ﴿١﴾

اَلَّا تَعۡبُدُوۡۤا اِلَّا اللّٰهَ ؕ اِنَّنِيۡ لَـكُمۡ مِّنۡهُ

نَذِيۡرٌ وَّبَشِيۡرٌ ۙ ﴿٢﴾

Can, then, (he
who cares for no more
than the life of this world
be compared with one who
takes his stand on a clear evidence
from his Sustainer (Rabb), conveyed
through (this Quran) testimony from
Him,as was the revelation vouchsafed
to Moses afore-time (a divine writ
ordained by Him) to be a guidance and
grace (unto man)? They (who understand
this message-it is they alone who truly)
believe in it; whereas for any of those who,
joined together (in common hostility),
deny its truth - the fire shall be their
appointed state (in the life to come).
And so,be not in doubt about this
(revelation): behold, it is the truth
from thy Sustainer, even though
most people will not believe
in it.

11:17

اَفَمَنْ كَانَ عَلٰى بَيِّنَةٍ مِّنْ رَّبِّهٖ
وَيَتْلُوْهُ شَاهِدٌ مِّنْهُ وَمِنْ قَبْلِهٖ
كِتٰبُ مُوْسٰٓى اِمَامًا وَّرَحْمَةً ؕ
اُولٰٓئِكَ يُؤْمِنُوْنَ بِهٖ ؕ وَمَنْ يَّكْفُرْ
بِهٖ مِنَ الْاَحْزَابِ فَالنَّارُ مَوْعِدُهٗ ۚ
فَلَا تَكُ فِيْ مِرْيَةٍ مِّنْهُ ۗ اِنَّهُ الْحَقُّ
مِنْ رَّبِّكَ وَلٰكِنَّ اَكْثَرَ النَّاسِ
لَا يُؤْمِنُوْنَ ﴿١٧﴾

Alif. Lam. Ra. These are messages of a revelation clear in itself and clearly showing the truth

12:1

الٓرٰ ۫قف تِلۡكَ اٰيٰتُ الۡكِتٰبِ الۡمُبِيۡنِ ۫قف ﴿١﴾

Behold, We have bestowed it from
on high as a discourse in the Arabic
tongue, so that you might encompass it
with your reason.

12:2

اِنَّآ اَنْزَلْنٰهُ قُرْءٰنًا عَرَبِيًّا لَّعَلَّكُمْ
تَعْقِلُوْنَ ﴿٢﴾

In the measure that We revealt his Quran unto thee, (O Prophet,) We explain it to thee in the best possible way, seeing that before this you were indeed among those who are unaware (of what revelation is).

12:3

نَحْنُ نَقُصُّ عَلَيْكَ اَحْسَنَ الْقَصَصِ
بِمَآ اَوْحَيْنَآ اِلَيْكَ هٰذَا الْقُرْاٰنَ ۖ وَ
اِنْ كُنْتَ مِنْ قَبْلِهٖ لَمِنَ الْغٰفِلِيْنَ ﴿٣﴾

There is, in their stories, instruction for men who have understanding. It is not a tale invented, but a confirmation of what went before it-a detailed exposition of all things, and a Guide and a Mercy to those who believe in it.

12:111

لَقَدْ كَانَ فِيْ قَصَصِهِمْ عِبْرَةٌ لِّاُوْلِي
الْاَلْبٰبِ ؕ مَا كَانَ حَدِيْثًا يُّفْتَرٰى
وَلٰكِنْ تَصْدِيْقَ الَّذِىْ بَيْنَ يَدَيْهِ
وَتَفْصِيْلَ كُلِّ شَىْءٍ وَّهُدًى وَّرَحْمَةً
لِّقَوْمٍ يُّؤْمِنُوْنَ ﴿١١١﴾ ع

Alif. Lam. Mim. Ra. These are messages of Revelation: and what has been bestowed upon you from on high by your Sustainer is the truth-yet most people will not believe (in it)?

13:1

الٓمّٓرٰ قف تِلْكَ اٰيٰتُ الْكِتٰبِ ط وَالَّذِيْٓ
اُنْزِلَ اِلَيْكَ مِنْ رَّبِّكَ الْحَقُّ وَلٰكِنَّ
اَكْثَرَ النَّاسِ لَا يُؤْمِنُوْنَ ﴿١﴾

Yet even if (they
should listen to) a
(Divine) discourse by
which mountains could be
moved, or the earth cleft asunder,
or the dead made to speak - (they
who are bent on denying the truth
would still refuse to believe in it)! No,
but Allah alone has the power to decide
what shall be. Have, then, they who
have attained to faith not yet come to
know that, had Allah so willed; He would
indeed have guided all mankind aright?
But as for those who are bent on denying
the truth-in result of their (evil) deeds,
sudden calamities will always befall
them or will alight close to their
homes;(and this will continue) until
Allah's promise (of resurrection)
is fulfilled: Surely, Allah never
fails to fulfill His promise!

13:31

وَلَوْ اَنَّ قُرْاٰنًا سُيِّرَتْ
بِهِ الْجِبَالُ اَوْ قُطِّعَتْ بِهِ
الْاَرْضُ اَوْ كُلِّمَ بِهِ الْمَوْتٰى ط
بَلْ لِّلّٰهِ الْاَمْرُ جَمِيْعًا ط اَفَلَمْ يَايْئَسِ
الَّذِيْنَ اٰمَنُوْٓا اَنْ لَّوْ يَشَآءُ اللّٰهُ لَهَدَى
النَّاسَ جَمِيْعًا ط وَلَا يَزَالُ الَّذِيْنَ
كَفَرُوْا تُصِيْبُهُمْ بِمَا صَنَعُوْا
قَارِعَةٌ اَوْ تَحُلُّ قَرِيْبًا مِّنْ دَارِهِمْ
حَتّٰى يَاْتِيَ وَعْدُ اللّٰهِ ط اِنَّ اللّٰهَ لَا
يُخْلِفُ الْمِيْعَادَ ع ﴿٣١﴾

Thus have We revealed it (Quran) to be a judgment of authority in Arabic. If you follow their (vain) desires after the knowledge which has reached you, then you would find neither protector nor defender besides Allah.

13:37

وَكَذٰلِكَ اَنْزَلْنٰهُ حُكْمًا عَرَبِيًّا ؕ
وَلَىِٕنِ اتَّبَعْتَ اَهْوَآءَهُمْ بَعْدَ مَا
جَآءَكَ مِنَ الْعِلْمِ ۙ مَا لَكَ مِنَ اللّٰهِ مِنْ
وَّلِيٍّ وَّلَا وَاقٍ ﴿۳۷﴾ ع

Alif. Laam. Ra. A Book which We have revealed to you, in order that you may lead mankind out of the depths of darkness into light - by the leave of their Sustainer - to the Way of (Him) the Exalted in power, worthy of all praise.

14:1

الٓرٰ ۚ قف كِتٰبٌ اَنْزَلْنٰهُ اِلَيْكَ لِتُخْرِجَ
النَّاسَ مِنَ الظُّلُمٰتِ اِلَى النُّوْرِ ۙ۵ لا بِاِذْنِ
رَبِّهِمْ اِلٰى صِرٰطِ الْعَزِيْزِ الْحَمِيْدِ ۙ لا ﴿١﴾

Alif. Lam. Ra. These are messages of Revelation – of a discourse clear in itself and clearly showing the truth: And it will come to pass that those who are (now) bent on denying this truth will wish that they had surrendered themselves to God (in their life time).

15:1, 2

الٓرٰ قف تِلۡكَ اٰيٰتُ الۡكِتٰبِ وَ قُرۡاٰنٍ
مُّبِيۡنٍ ﴿۱﴾ رُبَمَا يَوَدُّ الَّذِيۡنَ كَفَرُوۡا
لَوۡ كَانُوۡا مُسۡلِمِيۡنَ ﴿۲﴾

Behold, it is We Ourselves who have bestowed from on high, step by step, this reminder? (Quran) and, behold, it is We who shall truly guard it (from all corruption).

15:9

إِنَّا نَحۡنُ نَزَّلۡنَا ٱلذِّكۡرَ وَإِنَّا لَهُۥ
لَحَٰفِظُونَ ٩

And, indeed, We have bestowed upon you seven of the oft repeated (verses), and (have, thus, laid open before thee) this sublime Quran:

15:87

وَلَقَدْ اٰتَيْنٰكَ سَبْعًا مِّنَ الْمَثَانِيْ وَ
الْقُرْاٰنَ الْعَظِيْمَ ﴿٨٧﴾

And say: "I am indeed he that warns openly and without ambiguity," (Of just such wrath) as We sent down on those who divided (Scripture into arbitrary parts), (and) who (now) declare this Quran to be (a tissue of) falsehoods!

15:89, 90, 91

وَقُلْ اِنِّيْٓ اَنَا النَّذِيْرُ الْمُبِيْنُ ﴿٨٩﴾ج كَمَآ
اَنْزَلْنَا عَلَى الْمُقْتَسِمِيْنَ ﴿٩٠﴾لا الَّذِيْنَ
جَعَلُوا الْقُرْاٰنَ عِضِيْنَ ﴿٩١﴾

And We sent down the Book to you for the express purpose, that thou should make clear to them those things in which they differ, and that it should be a Guide and a Mercy to those who believe.

16:64

وَ مَآ اَنْزَلْنَا عَلَيْكَ الْكِتٰبَ اِلَّا
لِتُبَيِّنَ لَهُمُ الَّذِى اخْتَلَفُوْا فِيْهِ ۙ وَ
هُدًى وَّ رَحْمَةً لِّقَوْمٍ يُّؤْمِنُوْنَ ﴿٦٤﴾

One day We shall raise from all Peoples a witness against them, from amongst themselves: and We shall bring thee as a witness against these (thy people): and We have sent down to you the Book explaining all things, a Guide, a Mercy, and Glad Tidings to Muslims (those who submit).

16:89

وَ يَوْمَ نَبْعَثُ فِيْ كُلِّ اُمَّةٍ شَهِيْدًا
عَلَيْهِمْ مِّنْ اَنْفُسِهِمْ وَ جِئْنَا بِكَ
شَهِيْدًا عَلٰى هٰٓؤُلَآءِ ؕ وَ نَزَّلْنَا عَلَيْكَ
الْكِتٰبَ تِبْيَانًا لِّكُلِّ شَيْءٍ وَّ هُدًى وَّ
رَحْمَةً وَّ بُشْرٰى لِلْمُسْلِمِيْنَ ﴿٨٩﴾ ع

Now whenever you happen to read this Quran, seek refuge with Allah from Satan, the accursed.

16:98

فَإِذَا قَرَأْتَ الْقُرْآنَ فَاسْتَعِذْ بِاللَّهِ مِنَ
الشَّيْطَانِ الرَّجِيمِ ﴿٩٨﴾

Say, the Holy Spirit has brought
the Revelation from your Sustainer
(Rabb) in Truth, in order to strengthen
those who believe, and as a Guide
and Glad Tidings to Muslims (those
who submit).

16:102

قُلْ نَزَّلَهُ رُوحُ الْقُدُسِ مِنْ رَّبِّكَ
بِالْحَقِّ لِيُثَبِّتَ الَّذِينَ آمَنُوا وَهُدًى
وَّبُشْرَى لِلْمُسْلِمِينَ ﴿١٠٢﴾

And, indeed, full well do We know that they say, "It is but a human being that imparts all this to him!- (Notwithstanding that) the tongue of him to whom they so maliciously point is wholly outlandish,whereas this is Arabic speech, clear in itself and clearly showing the truth of its source.

16:103

وَ لَقَدۡ نَعۡلَمُ اَنَّهُمۡ يَقُوۡلُوۡنَ اِنَّمَا
يُعَلِّمُهٗ بَشَرٌ ؕ لِسَانُ الَّذِىۡ يُلۡحِدُوۡنَ
اِلَيۡهِ اَعۡجَمِىٌّ وَّهٰذَا لِسَانٌ عَرَبِىٌّ
مُّبِيۡنٌ ﴿١٠٣﴾

Surely this Quran does guide
to that which is most right (or
stable), and gives the glad tidings
to the Believers who work deeds of
righteousness, that they shall have
a magnificent reward; And to those
who believe not in the Hereafter, (it
announces) that We have prepared for
them a grievous penalty (indeed).

17:9, 10

اِنَّ هٰذَا الْقُرْاٰنَ يَهْدِىْ لِلَّتِىْ
هِىَ اَقْوَمُ وَيُبَشِّرُ الْمُؤْمِنِيْنَ
الَّذِيْنَ يَعْمَلُوْنَ الصّٰلِحٰتِ اَنَّ
لَهُمْ اَجْرًا كَبِيْرًا ۙ﴿٩﴾ وَّاَنَّ الَّذِيْنَ لَا
يُؤْمِنُوْنَ بِالْاٰخِرَةِ اَعْتَدْنَا لَهُمْ
عَذَابًا اَلِيْمًا ﴿١٠﴾ ع

And, indeed, many facets have We given (to Our message) in this Quran, so that they (who deny the truth) might take it to heart: but all this only increases their aversion.

17:41

وَلَقَدْ صَرَّفْنَا فِیْ هٰذَا الْقُرْاٰنِ لِیَذَّكَّرُوْا ؕ
وَمَا یَزِیْدُهُمْ اِلَّا نُفُوْرًا ﴿۴۱﴾

But (thus it is:) whenever you recite the Quran, We place an invisible barrier between you and those who will not believe in the life to come:

17:45

وَ اِذَا قَرَاْتَ الْقُرْاٰنَ جَعَلْنَا بَيْنَكَ
وَ بَيْنَ الَّذِيْنَ لَا يُؤْمِنُوْنَ بِالْاٰخِرَةِ
حِجَابًا مَّسْتُوْرًا ﴿۴۵﴾ لا

For, over their hearts We have laid veils which prevent them from grasping its purport, and into their ears, deafness. And so, whenever you do mention, while reciting the Quran, your Sustainer as the one and only Divine Being, they turn their backs (upon you) in aversion.

17:46

وَّجَعَلْنَا عَلٰى قُلُوْبِهِمْ اَكِنَّةً اَنْ
يَّفْقَهُوْهُ وَفِيْٓ اٰذَانِهِمْ وَقْرًا ۭ وَاِذَا
ذَكَرْتَ رَبَّكَ فِي الْقُرْاٰنِ وَحْدَهٗ وَلَّوْا
عَلٰٓي اَدْبَارِهِمْ نُفُوْرًا ۝٤٦

We send down (stage by stage) in the Quran that which is a healing and a Mercy to those who believe: to the unjust it causes nothing but loss after loss.

17:82

وَنُنَزِّلُ مِنَ الْقُرْاٰنِ مَا هُوَ شِفَآءٌ
وَّرَحْمَةٌ لِّلْمُؤْمِنِيْنَ ۙ وَلَا يَزِيْدُ
الظّٰلِمِيْنَ اِلَّا خَسَارًا ﴿٨٢﴾

Say: If all mankind and all invisible beings would come together with a view to producing the like of this Quran, they could not produce its like even though they were to exert all their strength in aiding one another!"

17:88

قُلْ لَّىِٕنِ اجْتَمَعَتِ الْاِنْسُ وَالْجِنُّ
عَلٰٓى اَنْ يَّاْتُوْا بِمِثْلِ هٰذَا الْقُرْاٰنِ
لَا يَاْتُوْنَ بِمِثْلِهٖ وَلَوْ كَانَ بَعْضُهُمْ
لِبَعْضٍ ظَهِيْرًا ﴿٨٨﴾

And We have explained to man, in this Quran, every kind of similitude: yet the greater part of men refuse (to receive it) except with ingratitude!

17:89

وَلَقَدْ صَرَّفْنَا لِلنَّاسِ فِیْ هٰذَا الْقُرْاٰنِ
مِنْ كُلِّ مَثَلٍ ۫ فَاَبٰۤی اَكْثَرُ النَّاسِ اِلَّا
كُفُوْرًا ﴿۸۹﴾

And aṣ a guide towards the
truth have We bestowed this
(Quran) from on high; with this
(very) truth has it come down (unto
you, O Messenger):for We have sent
you but as a herald of glad news and
a warner, (bearing) a discourse which
We have gradually unfolded, so that
thou might read it out to mankind in
stages, seeing that We have bestowed
it from on high step by step, as (one)
Revelation.

17:105, 106

وَ بِالْحَقِّ اَنْزَلْنٰهُ وَ بِالْحَقِّ نَزَلَ ؕ وَ مَآ
اَرْسَلْنٰكَ اِلَّا مُبَشِّرًا وَّ نَذِيْرًا ﴿١٠٥﴾
وَ قُرْاٰنًا فَرَقْنٰهُ لِتَقْرَاَهٗ عَلَى النَّاسِ عَلٰى
مُكْثٍ وَّ نَزَّلْنٰهُ تَنْزِيْلًا ﴿١٠٦﴾

Say: Believe in it or do not believe. Behold, those who are already endowed with knowledge fall down upon their faces in prostration as soon as this (Quran) is conveyed to them,

17:107

قُلْ اٰمِنُوْا بِهٖۤ اَوْلَا تُؤْمِنُوْا ؕ اِنَّ
الَّذِيْنَ اُوْتُوا الْعِلْمَ مِنْ قَبْلِهٖۤ اِذَا يُتْلٰى
عَلَيْهِمْ يَخِرُّوْنَ لِلْاَذْقَانِ سُجَّدًا ۙ ۱۰۷

All praise is due to Allah, Who has revealed this Divine Book (Quran) from on high upon His servant, and has not allowed any deviousness to obscure its meaning.

18:1

اَلۡحَمۡدُ لِلّٰهِ الَّذِیۡۤ اَنۡزَلَ عَلٰی عَبۡدِهِ

الۡكِتٰبَ وَلَمۡ یَجۡعَلۡ لَّهٗ عِوَجًا ؕ سکتة ﴿۱﴾

And convey (to the world) whatever has been revealed to you (O Muhammad) of your Sustainer's book (Quran). There is nothing that could alter His words; and you cannot find any refuge other than with Him.

18:27

وَاتْلُ مَآ اُوْحِيَ اِلَيْكَ مِنْ كِتَابِ

رَبِّكَ ۚ لَا مُبَدِّلَ لِكَلِمٰتِهٖ ۚ وَلَنْ تَجِدَ

مِنْ دُوْنِهٖ مُلْتَحَدًا ﴿٢٧﴾

We have explained in detail in this Quran, for the benefit of mankind, every kind of similitude: but man is, in most things, given to contentions (controversies).

18:54

وَلَقَدْ صَرَّفْنَا فِىْ هٰذَا الْقُرْاٰنِ لِلنَّاسِ
مِنْ كُلِّ مَثَلٍ ؕ وَكَانَ الْاِنْسٰنُ اَكْثَرَ
شَیْءٍ جَدَلًا ﴿۵۴﴾

We did not reveal the Quran on you to make you unhappy, but only as a communication to urge all who fear Allah.

20:2, 3

مَآ اَنْزَلْنَا عَلَيْكَ الْقُرْاٰنَ لِتَشْقٰٓى ﴿٢﴾ لا
اِلَّا تَذْكِرَةً لِّمَنْ يَّخْشٰى ﴿٣﴾ لا

And thus have We bestowed from on high this (Quran) as a discourse in the Arabic tongue, and have given therein many facets (similitudes) to all manner of warnings, so that men might remain conscious of Us, or that it give rise to a new awareness in them.

20:113

وَكَذٰلِكَ اَنْزَلْنٰهُ قُرْاٰنًا عَرَبِيًّا وَّ
صَرَّفْنَا فِيْهِ مِنَ الْوَعِيْدِ لَعَلَّهُمْ
يَتَّقُوْنَ اَوْ يُحْدِثُ لَهُمْ ذِكْرًا ﴿١١٣﴾

(Know,) then, (that) Allah is sublimely exalted, the Ultimate Sovereign, the Ultimate Truth and (knowing this,) do not approach the Quran in haste, before it has been revealed unto you in full, but (always) say: "O my Sustainer (Rabb), cause me to grow in knowledge!

20:114

فَتَعٰلَى اللّٰهُ الْمَلِكُ الْحَقُّ ۚ وَلَا تَعْجَلْ
بِالْقُرْاٰنِ مِنْ قَبْلِ اَنْ يُّقْضٰٓى اِلَيْكَ
وَحْيُهٗ ۫ وَقُلْ رَّبِّ زِدْنِىْ عِلْمًا ﴿١١٤﴾

We have revealed for you (O men!) a book in which is a Message for you: will you not then understand?

21:10

لَقَدْ اَنْزَلْنَاۤ اِلَيْكُمْ كِتٰبًا فِيْهِ
ذِكْرُكُمْ ؕ اَفَلَا تَعْقِلُوْنَ ۧ ﴿۱۰﴾

Or have they taken for worship (other) gods besides Him? Say, "Bring your convincing proof: this is the Message of those with me and the Message of those before me." But most of them know not the Truth, and so turn away.

21:24

اَمِ اتَّخَذُوْا مِنْ دُوْنِهٖۤ اٰلِهَةً ؕ قُلْ
هَاتُوْا بُرْهٰنَكُمْ ۚ هٰذَا ذِكْرُ مَنْ
مَّعِیَ وَ ذِكْرُ مَنْ قَبْلِیْ ؕ بَلْ اَكْثَرُهُمْ
لَا یَعْلَمُوْنَ ۙ الْحَقَّ فَهُمْ مُّعْرِضُوْنَ ﴿۲۴﴾

And (like those earlier Revelations,) this one, too, is a blessed Reminder which We have bestowed from on high: will you, then, reject it?

21:50

وَهٰذَا ذِكْرٌ مُّبَارَكٌ اَنْزَلْنٰهُ ؕ اَفَاَنْتُمْ
لَهٗ مُنْكِرُوْنَ ﴿۵۰﴾ ع

Herein, behold, there is a message for people who (truly) obey Allah.

21:106

إِنَّ فِي هَٰذَا لَبَلَٰغًا لِّقَوْمٍ عَٰبِدِينَ ۝١٠٦

And among mankind is he who disputes concerning Allah without knowledge or guidance or a Scripture giving light.

22:8

وَ مِنَ النَّاسِ مَنْ يُّجَادِلُ فِى اللّٰهِ بِغَيْرِ
عِلْمٍ وَّ لَا هُدًى وَّ لَا كِتٰبٍ مُّنِيْرٍ ﴿۸﴾

If the Truth had been in accord with their desires, truly heavens and earth and all beings therein would have been brought to ruin. Rather We have brought them their Reminder, but they keep on avoiding their Reminder.

23:71

وَلَوِ اتَّبَعَ الْحَقُّ اَهْوَآءَهُمْ لَفَسَدَتِ
السَّمٰوٰتُ وَالْاَرْضُ وَمَنْ فِيْهِنَّ ؕ
بَلْ اَتَيْنٰهُمْ بِذِكْرِهِمْ فَهُمْ عَنْ
ذِكْرِهِمْ مُّعْرِضُوْنَ ؕ ﴿٧١﴾

We have sent them the Truth: but they indeed practise falsehood!

23:90

بَلْ اَتَيْنٰهُمْ بِالْحَقِّ وَ اِنَّهُمْ لَكٰذِبُوْنَ ﴿٩٠﴾

A Surah (is this) which We have bestowed from on high, and which We have laid down in plain terms; and in it have We bestowed from on high messages which are clear (in themselves), so that you might keep (them) in mind.

24:1

سُوْرَةٌ اَنْزَلْنٰهَا وَفَرَضْنٰهَا وَاَنْزَلْنَا
فِيْهَاۤ اٰيٰتٍۭ بَيِّنٰتٍ لَّعَلَّكُمْ تَذَكَّرُوْنَ ﴿١﴾

The answer of the Believers, when summoned to Allah and His Messenger, in order that He may judge between them, is no other than this: they say, "We hear and we obey": These people will flourish and live a happy and successful life.

24:51

اِنَّمَا كَانَ قَوْلَ الْمُؤْمِنِيْنَ اِذَا دُعُوْٓا
اِلَى اللّٰهِ وَ رَسُوْلِهٖ لِيَحْكُمَ بَيْنَهُمْ اَنْ
يَّقُوْلُوْا سَمِعْنَا وَ اَطَعْنَا ؕ وَ اُولٰٓئِكَ
هُمُ الْمُفْلِحُوْنَ ﴿۵۱﴾

Say (O Muhammad): "He who knows all the mysteries of the heavens and the earth has bestowed from on high this (Quran upon me)! Surely, He is much-forgiving, a dispenser of grace!"

25:6

قُلْ اَنْزَلَهُ الَّذِىْ يَعْلَمُ السِّـرَّ فِى
السَّـمٰوٰتِ وَ الْاَرْضِ ؕ اِنَّهٗ كَانَ
غَفُوْرًا رَّحِيْمًا ﴿٦﴾

And (on that Day) the Apostle will say: "O my Sustainer (Rabb)! Behold, (some of) my people have come to regard this Quran as something that ought to be discarded!"

25:30

وَقَالَ الرَّسُوۡلُ یٰرَبِّ اِنَّ قَوۡمِی
اتَّخَذُوۡا هٰذَا الۡقُرۡاٰنَ مَهۡجُوۡرًا ﴿۳۰﴾

Now they who are bent
on denying the truth are
in the habit to ask. "Why has
not the Quran been bestowed
on him from on high in one single
revelation?" (It has been revealed)
in this manner so that We might
strengthen your heart thereby–for
We have so arranged its component
parts that they form one consistent
whole and (that) they (who deny the
truth) might never taunt you with any
deceptive half-truth without Our
conveying to you the (full) truth
and (providing you) with the
best explanation.

25:32, 33

وَ قَالَ الَّذِيْنَ كَفَرُوْا لَوْلَا نُزِّلَ عَلَيْهِ
الْقُرْاٰنُ جُمْلَةً وَّاحِدَةً ۛ كَذٰلِكَ ۛ
لِنُثَبِّتَ بِهٖ فُؤَادَكَ وَرَتَّلْنٰهُ تَرْتِيْلًا ﴿٣٢﴾
وَلَا يَاْتُوْنَكَ بِمَثَلٍ اِلَّا جِئْنٰكَ بِالْحَقِّ
وَاَحْسَنَ تَفْسِيْرًا ﴿٣٣﴾ ط

These are Messeges of the Divine writ (Quran), clear in itself and clearly showing the truth!

26:2

تِلۡكَ ءَايَٰتُ ٱلۡكِتَٰبِ ٱلۡمُبِينِ ﴿٢﴾

Now, behold, this (Quran) has indeed been bestowed from on high by the Sustainer (Rabb) of all the worlds trustworthy Divine inspiration has alighted with it from on highupon thy heart, (O Muhammad) so that you may be among those who preach in the clear Arabic tongue.

26:192, 193, 194, 195

وَاِنَّهٗ لَتَنْزِيْلُ رَبِّ الْعٰلَمِيْنَ ﴿۱۹۲﴾ ط
نَزَلَ بِهِ الرُّوْحُ الْاَمِيْنُ ﴿۱۹۳﴾ لا عَلٰى
قَلْبِكَ لِتَكُوْنَ مِنَ الْمُنْذِرِيْنَ ﴿۱۹۴﴾ لا
بِلِسَانٍ عَرَبِيٍّ مُّبِيْنٍ ﴿۱۹۵﴾ ط

And, surely, (the essence of) this Quran is indeed found in the ancient books of Divine wisdom as well. Is it not evidence enough for them that so many learned men from among the children of Israel have recognized this (as true)?

26:196, 197

وَاِنَّهٗ لَفِیْ زُبُرِ الْاَوَّلِیْنَ ﴿۱۹۶﴾ اَوَلَمْ
یَکُنْ لَّهُمْ اٰیَةً اَنْ یَّعْلَمَهٗ عُلَمٰٓؤُا بَنِیْٓ
اِسْرَآءِیْلَ ﴿۱۹۷﴾ؕ

But even had We bestowed it from on high upon any of the non-Arabs, and had he recited it to them in his own tongue, they would not have believed in it.

26:198, 199

وَلَوْ نَزَّلْنٰهُ عَلٰى بَعْضِ الْاَعْجَمِيْنَ ﴿۱۹۸﴾ لا

فَقَرَاَهٗ عَلَيْهِمْ مَّا كَانُوْا بِهٖ مُؤْمِنِيْنَ ﴿۱۹۹﴾ ط

No evil ones have brought down this (Revelation):

26:210

وَمَا تَنَزَّلَتْ بِهِ الشَّيٰطِينُ ﴿٢١٠﴾ ج

Ta. Sin. These are verses of the Quran–a book that makes (things) clear; A guide: and glad tidings for the believers. Those who establish regular prayers and give in regular charity, and also have (full) assurance of the hereafter.

27:1, 2, 3

طٰسٓ ۚ قف تِلْكَ اٰيٰتُ الْقُرْاٰنِ وَكِتَابٍ
مُّبِيْنٍ ۙ ﴿١﴾ هُدًى وَّبُشْرٰى لِلْمُؤْمِنِيْنَ ۙ ﴿٢﴾
الَّذِيْنَ يُقِيْمُوْنَ الصَّلٰوةَ وَيُؤْتُوْنَ
الزَّكٰوةَ وَهُمْ بِالْاٰخِرَةِ هُمْ يُوْقِنُوْنَ ﴿٣﴾

Behold, this Quran explains to
the children of Israel most of that
whereon they hold divergent views;
and it certainly is a Guide and a Mercy
to those who believe.

27:76, 77

اِنَّ هٰذَا الْقُرْاٰنَ يَقُصُّ عَلٰى بَنِيْٓ
اِسْرَآءِيْلَ اَكْثَرَ الَّذِيْ هُمْ فِيْهِ
يَخْتَلِفُوْنَ ﴿٧٦﴾ وَاِنَّهٗ لَهُدًى وَّرَحْمَةٌ
لِّلْمُؤْمِنِيْنَ ﴿٧٧﴾

And to convey this Quran to the world. Whoever, therefore, chooses to follow the right path, follows it but for his own good; and if any wills to go astray, say to him: “I am only a warner.”

27:92

وَ اَنْ اَتْلُوَا الْقُرْاٰنَ ۚ فَمَنِ اهْتَدٰى
فَاِنَّمَا يَهْتَدِىْ لِنَفْسِهٖ ۚ وَمَنْ ضَلَّ
فَقُلْ اِنَّمَآ اَنَا مِنَ الْمُنْذِرِيْنَ ﴿٩٢﴾

These are messages of a Divine writ (Quran) clear in itself and clearly showing the truth.

28:2

تِلۡكَ ءَايَٰتُ ٱلۡكِتَٰبِ ٱلۡمُبِينِ ٢

Say: "Then bring you a Book from Allah, which is a better guide than either of them, that I may follow it! (do), if ye are truthful. But if they do not listen to you, know that they only follow their own lusts and desires: and who is more astray than one who follows his own lusts and desires, devoid of guidance from Allah. Allah does not guide people given to wrong-doing.

28:49, 50

قُلْ فَأْتُوْا بِكِتٰبٍ مِّنْ عِنْدِ
اللّٰهِ هُوَ اَهْدٰى مِنْهُمَآ اَتَّبِعْهُ
اِنْ كُنْتُمْ صٰدِقِيْنَ ﴿٤٩﴾ فَاِنْ لَّمْ
يَسْتَجِيْبُوْا لَكَ فَاعْلَمْ اَنَّمَا يَتَّبِعُوْنَ
اَهْوَآءَهُمْ ؕ وَمَنْ اَضَلُّ مِمَّنِ اتَّبَعَ
هَوٰىهُ بِغَيْرِ هُدًى مِّنَ اللّٰهِ ؕ اِنَّ اللّٰهَ
لَا يَهْدِى الْقَوْمَ الظّٰلِمِيْنَ ﴿٥٠﴾ ع

Now, indeed, We have caused this word (of Ours) to reach mankind step by step, so that they might (learn to) keep it in mind.

28:51

وَلَقَدْ وَصَّلْنَا لَهُمُ الْقَوْلَ لَعَلَّهُمْ
يَتَذَكَّرُونَ ﴿٥١﴾

Convey to others whatever of this Divine writ (Quran) has been revealed to you,and be constant in prayer: for, behold, prayer restrains (man) from loathsome deeds and from all that runs counter to reason;and remembrance of Allah is indeed the greatest good. And Allah knows all that you do.

29:45

اُتْلُ مَآ اُوْحِیَ اِلَیْكَ مِنَ الْكِتٰبِ
وَاَقِمِ الصَّلٰوةَ ؕ اِنَّ الصَّلٰوةَ
تَنْهٰی عَنِ الْفَحْشَآءِ وَالْمُنْكَرِ ؕ
وَلَذِكْرُ اللّٰهِ اَكْبَرُ ؕ وَاللّٰهُ یَعْلَمُ مَا
تَصْنَعُوْنَ ﴿۴۵﴾

Is it not enough for them that We have sent down to you the Book (Quran) which is read to them? In this surely there is blessing, mercy, and a reminder for those who believe.

29:51

اَوَلَمۡ يَكۡفِهِمۡ اَنَّاۤ اَنۡزَلۡنَا عَلَيۡكَ
الۡكِتٰبَ يُتۡلٰى عَلَيۡهِمۡ ؕ اِنَّ فِىۡ ذٰلِكَ
لَرَحۡمَةً وَّذِكۡرٰى لِقَوۡمٍ يُّؤۡمِنُوۡنَ ﴿٥١﴾ ع

In this Quran We have put forth all kinds of parables (in many different ways); but whenever any Divine Law is presented to the people who have already decided not to accept the Message, they are sure to say that this is all a pack of lies and deceit.

30:58

وَلَقَدْ ضَرَبْنَا لِلنَّاسِ فِيْ هٰذَا الْقُرْاٰنِ
مِنْ كُلِّ مَثَلٍ ۭ وَلَىِٕنْ جِئْتَهُمْ بِاٰيَةٍ
لَّيَقُوْلَنَّ الَّذِيْنَ كَفَرُوْٓا اِنْ اَنْتُمْ اِلَّا
مُبْطِلُوْنَ ۝٥٨

These are Verses of the Wise Book.
A Guide and a Mercy to the doers
of good.

31:2, 3

تِلْكَ اٰيٰتُ الْكِتٰبِ الْحَكِيْمِ ﴿۲﴾ لا

هُدًى وَّ رَحْمَةً لِّلْمُحْسِنِيْنَ ﴿۳﴾ لا

This book (Quran) has beyond all doubt been revealed from the Sustainer (Rabb) of the Universe.

32:2

تَنۡزِیۡلُ الۡکِتٰبِ لَا رَیۡبَ فِیۡہِ مِنۡ رَّبِّ
الۡعٰلَمِیۡنَ ؕ﴿۲﴾

And yet, they who are bent on denying the truth, assert, "(Muhammad) has invented it!" Nay, but it is the truth from thy Sustainer (Rabb), enabling thee to warn (this) people to whom no warner has come before thee, so that they might follow the right path.

32:3

اَمْ يَقُوْلُوْنَ افْتَرٰىهُ ۚ بَلْ هُوَ الْحَقُّ
مِنْ رَّبِّكَ لِتُنْذِرَ قَوْمًا مَّآ اٰتٰىهُمْ مِّنْ
نَّذِيْرٍ مِّنْ قَبْلِكَ لَعَلَّهُمْ يَهْتَدُوْنَ ﴿٣﴾

And follow (but) that which comes
to you through Revelation from your
Sustainer: for Allah is truly aware of all
that you do, (O men).

33:2

وَّاتَّبِعۡ مَا یُوۡحٰۤی اِلَیۡکَ مِنۡ رَّبِّکَ ؕ اِنَّ
اللّٰہَ کَانَ بِمَا تَعۡمَلُوۡنَ خَبِیۡرًا ۙ﴿۲﴾

And those to whom knowledge has come see that the (Revelation) sent down to you from your Sustainer (Rabb)–that is the Truth, and that it guides to the Path of the Exalted (in might), Worthy of all praise.

34:6

وَ يَرَى الَّذِيْنَ اُوْتُوا الْعِلْمَ الَّذِيْٓ
اُنْزِلَ اِلَيْكَ مِنْ رَّبِّكَ هُوَ الْحَقَّ ۙ وَ
يَهْدِيْٓ اِلٰى صِرٰطِ الْعَزِيْزِ الْحَمِيْدِ ۝٦

(It is) they who (truly) follow Allah's Revelation, and are constant in prayer, and spend on others, secretly and openly, out of what We provide for them as sustenance–it is they who may look forward to a bargain that can never fail.

35:29

اِنَّ الَّذِيْنَ يَتْلُوْنَ كِتٰبَ اللّٰهِ وَ
اَقَامُوا الصَّلٰوةَ وَ اَنْفَقُوْا مِمَّا
رَزَقْنٰهُمْ سِرًّا وَّ عَلَانِيَةً يَّرْجُوْنَ
تِجَارَةً لَّنْ تَبُوْرَ ۙ ﴿٢٩﴾

That which We have revealed to you of the Book (Quran) is the Truth, confirming what was revealed before it: for Allah is assuredly–with respect to His Servants–well acquainted and Fully Observant.

35:31

وَالَّذِیۡۤ اَوۡحَیۡنَاۤ اِلَیۡکَ مِنَ الۡکِتٰبِ
هُوَ الۡحَقُّ مُصَدِّقًا لِّمَا بَیۡنَ یَدَیۡهِ ؕ اِنَّ
اللّٰهَ بِعِبَادِهٖ لَخَبِیۡرٌۢ بَصِیۡرٌ ﴿۳۱﴾

Consider this Quran full of wisdom: You are indeed one of the Messengers. On a Straight Way.by virtue of what is being bestowed (Quran) from on high by the Almighty, the Dispenser of Grace; in order that you may admonish a people, whose fathers had received no admonition, and who therefore remain heedless of the Signs of Allah.

36:2, 3, 4, 5, 6

وَالْقُرْاٰنِ الْحَكِيْمِ ۙ﴿۲﴾ اِنَّكَ
لَمِنَ الْمُرْسَلِيْنَ ۙ﴿۳﴾ عَلٰى صِرٰطٍ
مُّسْتَقِيْمٍ ؕ﴿۴﴾ تَنْزِيْلَ الْعَزِيْزِ
الرَّحِيْمِ ۙ﴿۵﴾ لِتُنْذِرَ قَوْمًا مَّاۤ اُنْذِرَ
اٰبَآؤُهُمْ فَهُمْ غٰفِلُوْنَ ﴿۶﴾

And (thus it is:) We have not imparted to this (Messenger the gift of) poetry, nor would (poetry) have suited this (message): it is but a reminder and a Divine discourse, clear in itself and clearly showing the truth to the end that it may warn everyone who is alive (of heart), and that the word (of Allah) may bear witness against all who deny the truth.

36:69, 70

وَمَا عَلَّمْنٰهُ الشِّعْرَ وَمَا يَنْۢبَغِيْ
لَهٗ ؕ اِنْ هُوَ اِلَّا ذِكْرٌ وَّ قُرْاٰنٌ مُّبِيْنٌ ۙ﴿٦٩﴾
لِّيُنْذِرَ مَنْ كَانَ حَيًّا وَّ يَحِقَّ الْقَوْلُ
عَلَى الْكٰفِرِيْنَ ﴿٧٠﴾

(All this have We expounded in this) blessed Divine book which We have revealed to thee, (O Muhammad,) so that men may ponder over its messages, and that those who are endowed with insight may take them to heart.

38:29

كِتٰبٌ اَنْزَلْنٰهُ اِلَيْكَ مُبٰرَكٌ لِّيَدَّبَّرُوْٓا
اٰيٰتِهٖ وَلِيَتَذَكَّرَ اُولُوا الْاَلْبَابِ ﴿٢٩﴾

This (Quran) is no less than a Message to (all) the Worlds.

38:87

إِنۡ هُوَ إِلَّا ذِكۡرٞ لِّلۡعَٰلَمِينَ ۝٨٧

The revelation of this Book is from Allah, the Exalted in Power, full of Wisdom. Surely it is We Who have revealed the Book to you in Truth: so serve Allah, offering Him sincere devotion.

39:1, 2

تَنْزِيْلُ الْكِتٰبِ مِنَ اللّٰهِ الْعَزِيْزِ

الْحَكِيْمِ ۝١ اِنَّآ اَنْزَلْنَآ اِلَيْكَ

الْكِتٰبَ بِالْحَقِّ فَاعْبُدِ اللّٰهَ مُخْلِصًا

لَّهُ الدِّيْنَ ؕ ۝٢

Allah bestows from
on high the best of all
teachings in the shape of
a Divine Book (Quran) fully
consistent within itself, repeating
each statement (of the truth) in
manifold forms. No contradictions
or differences can be found in it.
(A Divine Book) whereat shiver the
skins of all who of their Sustainer
stand in awe: (but) in the end their
skins and their hearts do soften at
the remembrance of (the Grace of)
Allah. Such is Allah's Guidance: He
guides therewith him that wills
(to be guided) whereas he whom
Allah lets go astray can never
find any guide.

39:23

اَللّٰهُ نَزَّلَ اَحۡسَنَ الۡحَدِيۡثِ كِتٰبًا
مُّتَشٰبِهًا مَّثَانِىَ ۖ تَقۡشَعِرُّ مِنۡهُ
جُلُوۡدُ الَّذِيۡنَ يَخۡشَوۡنَ رَبَّهُمۡ ۚ ثُمَّ
تَلِيۡنُ جُلُوۡدُهُمۡ وَ قُلُوۡبُهُمۡ اِلٰى ذِكۡرِ
اللّٰهِ ؕ ذٰلِكَ هُدَى اللّٰهِ يَهۡدِىۡ بِهٖ مَنۡ
يَّشَآءُ ؕ وَ مَنۡ يُّضۡلِلِ اللّٰهُ فَمَا لَهٗ
مِنۡ هَادٍ ﴿۲۳﴾

We have put forth for men, in this Quran every kind of Parable (story with a moral) , in order that they may receive admonition.

39:27

وَ لَقَدۡ ضَرَبۡنَا لِلنَّاسِ فِیۡ هٰذَا
الۡقُرۡاٰنِ مِنۡ کُلِّ مَثَلٍ لَّعَلَّهُمۡ
یَتَذَکَّرُوۡنَ ﴿ۚ۲۷﴾

Surely We have revealed the Book
to you in Truth, for (instructing)
mankind. He, then, that receives
guidance benefits his own soul: but he
that strays injures his own soul. You are
not their custodian.

39:41

اِنَّآ اَنْزَلْنَا عَلَيْكَ الْكِتٰبَ لِلنَّاسِ
بِالْحَقِّ ۚ فَمَنِ اهْتَدٰى فَلِنَفْسِهٖ ۚ
وَمَنْ ضَلَّ فَاِنَّمَا يَضِلُّ عَلَيْهَا ۚ وَمَآ
اَنْتَ عَلَيْهِمْ بِوَكِيْلٍ ﴿٤١﴾ ع

And before that suffering comes upon you all of a sudden, without your being aware (of its approach), follow the most goodly (teachings of the Quran) that has been revealed unto you by your Sustainer.

39:55

وَ اتَّبِعُوْٓا اَحْسَنَ مَآ اُنْزِلَ اِلَيْكُمْ
مِّنْ رَّبِّكُمْ مِّنْ قَبْلِ اَنْ يَّاْتِيَكُمُ
الْعَذَابُ بَغْتَةً وَّ اَنْتُمْ لَا تَشْعُرُوْنَ ۙ﴿۵۵﴾

The bestowal from on high of this Divine writ (Quran) issues from Allah, the Almighty, the All-Knowing,

40:2

تَنْزِيْلُ الْكِتٰبِ مِنَ اللّٰهِ الْعَزِيْزِ
الْعَلِيْمِ ﴿٢﴾ۙ

The bestowal from on high of this Revelation (Quran) issues from the Most Gracious, the Dispenser of Grace:

41:2

تَنۡزِيۡلٌ مِّنَ الرَّحۡمٰنِ الرَّحِيۡمِ ۚ﴿۲﴾

This is a Book, whereof the verses are explained in detail;–a Quran in Arabic, for people who understand; Giving good news and warning: yet most of them turn away, and so they do not hear.

41:3, 4

كِتٰبٌ فُصِّلَتْ اٰيٰتُهٗ قُرْاٰنًا عَرَبِيًّا
لِّقَوْمٍ يَّعْلَمُوْنَ ۙ﴿٣﴾ بَشِيْرًا وَّ نَذِيْرًا ۚ
فَاَعْرَضَ اَكْثَرُهُمْ فَهُمْ لَا يَسْمَعُوْنَ ﴿٤﴾

Now those who are bent on denying the truth say (unto one another): "Do not listen to this Quran, but rather talk frivolously about it, so that you might gain the upper hand!"

41:26

وَ قَالَ الَّذِيْنَ كَفَرُوْا لَا تَسْمَعُوْا
لِهٰذَا الْقُرْاٰنِ وَ الْغَوْا فِيْهِ لَعَلَّكُمْ
تَغْلِبُوْنَ ﴿٢٦﴾

Certainly, they who are bent on denying the truth of this reminder as soon as it comes to them–(they are the losers): for, behold, it is a sublime Divine Book. No falsehood can ever attain to it openly, and neither in a secret manner, (since it is) bestowed from on high by One who is truly Wise, ever to be praised.

41:41, 42

اِنَّ الَّذِيْنَ كَفَرُوْا بِالذِّكْرِ لَمَّا
جَآءَهُمْ ۚ وَاِنَّهٗ لَكِتٰبٌ عَزِيْزٌ ۙ ﴿٤١﴾
لَّا يَاْتِيْهِ الْبٰطِلُ مِنْۢ بَيْنِ يَدَيْهِ وَلَا
مِنْ خَلْفِهٖ ؕ تَنْزِيْلٌ مِّنْ حَكِيْمٍ
حَمِيْدٍ ﴿٤٢﴾

Had We sent this as a Quran
(in the language) other than
Arabic, they would have said:
"Why are not its verses explained in
detail? What! (a Book) not in Arabic
and (a Messenger an Arab?" Say: "It is
a Guide and a Healing to those who
believe; and for those who believe not,
there is a deafness in their ears, and it
is blindness in their (eyes): They are
(as it were) being called from a place
far distant!"

41:44

وَ لَوْ جَعَلْنٰهُ قُرْاٰنًا اَعْجَمِيًّا
لَّقَالُوْا لَوْ لَا فُصِّلَتْ اٰيٰتُهٗ ؕ ءَ
اَعْجَمِيٌّ وَّ عَرَبِيٌّ ؕ قُلْ هُوَ لِلَّذِيْنَ
اٰمَنُوْا هُدًى وَّ شِفَآءٌ ؕ وَ الَّذِيْنَ
لَا يُؤْمِنُوْنَ فِيْٓ اٰذَانِهِمْ وَقْرٌ وَّ هُوَ
عَلَيْهِمْ عَمًى ؕ اُولٰٓئِكَ يُنَادَوْنَ مِنْ
مَّكَانٍۭ بَعِيْدٍ ۝٤٤ ع

Thus have We sent by inspiration to you an Arabic Quran: that you may warn the Mother of Cities and all around her,–and warn (them) of the Day of Assembly, of which there is no doubt: (when) some will be in the Garden, and some in the Blazing Fire.

42:7

وَكَذٰلِكَ اَوْحَيْنَآ اِلَيْكَ قُرْاٰنًا
عَرَبِيًّا لِّتُنْذِرَ اُمَّ الْقُرٰى وَمَنْ
حَوْلَهَا وَتُنْذِرَ يَوْمَ الْجَمْعِ لَا
رَيْبَ فِيْهِ ؕ فَرِيْقٌ فِى الْجَنَّةِ وَفَرِيْقٌ
فِى السَّعِيْرِ ۝٧

Now then, for that (reason), call (them to the Faith), and stand steadfast as you are commanded, nor follow thou their vain desires; but say: "I believe in the Book which Allah has sent down; and I am commanded to judge justly between you. Allah is our Sustainer (Rabb) and your Sustainer (Rabb): for us (is the responsibility for) our deeds, and for you for your deeds. There is no conflict or dispute between us and you. Allah will bring us together, and to Him is (our) Final Goal.

42:15

فَلِذٰلِكَ فَادْعُ ۚ وَ اسْتَقِمْ كَمَآ
اُمِرْتَ ۚ وَلَا تَتَّبِعْ اَهْوَآءَهُمْ ۚ
وَ قُلْ اٰمَنْتُ بِمَآ اَنْزَلَ اللّٰهُ مِنْ
كِتٰبٍ ۚ وَ اُمِرْتُ لِاَعْدِلَ بَيْنَكُمْ ؕ
اَللّٰهُ رَبُّنَا وَ رَبُّكُمْ ؕ لَنَآ اَعْمٰلُنَا وَ
لَكُمْ اَعْمٰلُكُمْ ؕ لَا حُجَّةَ بَيْنَنَا وَ
بَيْنَكُمْ ؕ اَللّٰهُ يَجْمَعُ بَيْنَنَا ۚ وَ
اِلَيْهِ الْمَصِيْرُ ؕ ﴿١٥﴾

It is Allah Who has sent down the Book in Truth, and the Balance (by which to weigh conduct). And what will make thee realise that perhaps the Hour (Day of Judgment) is close at hand.

42:17

اَللّٰهُ الَّذِیۡۤ اَنۡزَلَ الۡکِتٰبَ بِالۡحَقِّ وَ
الۡمِیۡزَانَ ؕ وَمَا یُدۡرِیۡکَ لَعَلَّ السَّاعَۃَ
قَرِیۡبٌ ﴿۱۷﴾

And thus, too, (O Muhammad) have We revealed to you a life-giving message,(coming) at Our behest. Before this message came to you, ou did not know what revelation is, nor what faith implies: but (now) We have caused this (Quran) to be a light, whereby We guide whom We will of Our servants: and, surely, you too, shall guide (men) onto the straight way.

42:52

وَكَذٰلِكَ اَوْحَيْنَآ اِلَيْكَ رُوْحًا
مِّنْ اَمْرِنَا ؕ مَا كُنْتَ تَدْرِىْ
مَا الْكِتٰبُ وَلَا الْاِيْمٰنُ وَلٰكِنْ
جَعَلْنٰهُ نُوْرًا نَّهْدِىْ بِهٖ مَنْ نَّشَآءُ مِنْ
عِبَادِنَا ؕ وَاِنَّكَ لَتَهْدِىْٓ اِلٰى صِرٰطٍ
مُّسْتَقِيْمٍ ۙ ﴿۵۲﴾

Consider this Divine Book (Quran), clear in itself and clearly showing the truth. Behold, We have caused it to be a discourse in Arabic, so that you might understand it with your reason. And, surely, (originating as it does) in the source, with Us, of all Revelations, it is indeed Sublime, full of Wisdom.

43:2, 3, 4

وَ الۡكِتٰبِ الۡمُبِيۡنِ ۛۙ ﴿۲﴾ اِنَّا جَعَلۡنٰهُ قُرۡءٰنًا
عَرَبِيًّا لَّعَلَّكُمۡ تَعۡقِلُوۡنَ ۚ﴿۳﴾ وَ اِنَّهٗ فِيۡۤ اُمِّ
الۡكِتٰبِ لَدَيۡنَا لَعَلِيٌّ حَكِيۡمٌ ؕ﴿۴﴾

And, surely, this revelation (Quran)
shall indeed become (a source of)
eminence for you and your people: but
in time you all will be called to account
(for what you have done with it)

43:44

وَاِنَّهٗ لَذِكْرٌ لَّكَ وَلِقَوْمِكَ ۚ وَسَوْفَ
تُسْـَٔلُوْنَ ﴿۴۴﴾

Consider this Divine writ (Quran), clear in itself and clearly showing the truth! Behold, from on high have We bestowed it on a blessed night: for, verily, We have always been warning (man). On that (night) was made clear, in wisdom, the distinction between all things (good and evil).

44:2, 3, 4

وَ الْكِتٰبِ الْمُبِيْنِ ﴿٢﴾ اِنَّا اَنْزَلْنٰهُ فِيْ
لَيْلَةٍ مُّبٰرَكَةٍ اِنَّا كُنَّا مُنْذِرِيْنَ ﴿٣﴾ فِيْهَا
يُفْرَقُ كُلُّ اَمْرٍ حَكِيْمٍ ﴿٤﴾

At a behest from Ourselves:
for, surely, We have always been
sending Our messages of guidance in
pursuance of your Sustainer's Grace (to
man). Surely, He alone is all-hearing,
all-knowing,

44:5, 6

أَمْرًا مِّنْ عِنْدِنَا ؕ اِنَّا كُنَّا
مُرْسِلِيْنَ ۚ ﴿٥﴾ رَحْمَةً مِّنْ رَّبِّكَ ؕ اِنَّهٗ
هُوَ السَّمِيْعُ الْعَلِيْمُ ۙ ﴿٦﴾

Thus, then, (O Messenger,) We have made this (Quran) easy to understand in your own language, so that men might take it to heart.

44:58

فَإِنَّمَا يَسَّرْنَٰهُ بِلِسَانِكَ لَعَلَّهُمْ
يَتَذَكَّرُونَ ﴿٥٨﴾

The revelation of this Book is from Allah the Exalted in Power, Full of Wisdom.

45:2

تَنْزِيْلُ الْكِتٰبِ مِنَ اللّٰهِ الْعَزِيْزِ
الْحَكِيْمِ ﴿٢﴾

These are clear evidences to men and
a Guidance and Mercy to those of
assured Faith.

45:20

هَٰذَا بَصَٰٓئِرُ لِلنَّاسِ وَهُدًى وَرَحۡمَةٞ
لِّقَوۡمٖ يُوقِنُونَ ٢٠

The bestowal from on high of this
Divine writ (Quran) issues from Allah,
the Almighty, the Wise.

46:2

تَنْزِيْلُ الْكِتٰبِ مِنَ اللّٰهِ الْعَزِيْزِ
الْحَكِيْمِ ﴿٢﴾

Say: “Have you given thought
to how you will fare if this be
truly (a Revelation) from Allah
and yet you deny its truth?–even
though a witness from among the
children of Israel has already borne
witness to (the advent of) one like
himself,and has believed in him, the
while you glory in your arrogance (and
reject his message)? Verily, Allah does
not grace such evildoing folk with
His Guidance!”

46:10

قُلْ اَرَءَيْتُمْ اِنْ كَانَ مِنْ عِنْدِ
اللّٰهِ وَ كَفَرْتُمْ بِهٖ وَ شَهِدَ شَاهِدٌ
مِّنْۢ بَنِيْٓ اِسْرَآءِيْلَ عَلٰى مِثْلِهٖ فَاٰمَنَ
وَ اسْتَكْبَرْتُمْ ؕ اِنَّ اللّٰهَ لَا يَهْدِى
الْقَوْمَ الظّٰلِمِيْنَ ﴿١٠﴾ ع

And yet, before this there was the revelation of Moses, a guide and a (sign of Allah's) grace; and this (Quran) is a Divine writ confirming the truth of the Torahin the Arabic tongue, to warn those who are bent on evildoing, and to bring a glad tiding to the doers of good:

46:12

وَ مِنْ قَبْلِهٖ كِتٰبُ مُوْسٰٓى اِمَامًا
وَّ رَحْمَةً ؕ وَ هٰذَا كِتٰبٌ مُّصَدِّقٌ
لِّسَانًا عَرَبِيًّا لِّيُنْذِرَ الَّذِيْنَ ظَلَمُوْا ۖۗ
وَ بُشْرٰى لِلْمُحْسِنِيْنَ ۚ﴿۱۲﴾

And Lo! We caused a group of unseen beings to incline towards you, (O Muhammad,)so that they might give ear to the Quran; and so, as soon as they became aware of it, they said (to one another), "Listen in silence!" And when (the recitation) was ended, they returned to their people as warners.

46:29

وَاِذْ صَرَفْنَآ اِلَيْكَ نَفَرًا مِّنَ الْجِنِّ
يَسْتَمِعُوْنَ الْقُرْاٰنَ ۚ فَلَمَّا حَضَرُوْهُ
قَالُوْٓا اَنْصِتُوْا ۚ فَلَمَّا قُضِيَ وَلَّوْا اِلٰى
قَوْمِهِمْ مُّنْذِرِيْنَ ﴿٢٩﴾

They said: "O our people! Behold, we have been listening to a revelation bestowed from on high after (that of) Moses, confirming the truth of whatever there still remains (of the Torah): it guides towards the truth, and onto a straight way.

46:30

قَالُوْا يٰقَوْمَنَآ اِنَّا سَمِعْنَا كِتٰبًا
اُنْزِلَ مِنْۢ بَعْدِ مُوْسٰى مُصَدِّقًا لِّمَا بَيْنَ
يَدَيْهِ يَهْدِيْٓ اِلَى الْحَقِّ وَاِلٰى طَرِيْقٍ
مُّسْتَقِيْمٍ ﴿٣٠﴾

"O our people! Respond to Allah's call, and have faith in Him: He will forgive you (whatever is past) of your sins, and deliver you from grievous suffering (in the life to come.

46:31

يٰقَوْمَنَآ اَجِيْبُوْا دَاعِيَ اللّٰهِ وَ
اٰمِنُوْا بِهٖ يَغْفِرْ لَكُمْ مِّنْ ذُنُوْبِكُمْ وَ
يُجِرْكُمْ مِّنْ عَذَابٍ اَلِيْمٍ ﴿٣١﴾

But he who does not respond to God's call can never elude (Him) on earth, nor can he has any protector against Him (in the life to come): all such are most obviously lost in error.

46:32

وَمَنْ لَّا يُجِبْ دَاعِيَ اللّٰهِ فَلَيْسَ
بِمُعْجِزٍ فِي الْاَرْضِ وَلَيْسَ لَهٗ مِنْ دُوْنِهٖٓ
اَوْلِيَآءُ ؕ اُولٰٓئِكَ فِيْ ضَلٰلٍ مُّبِيْنٍ ﴿۳۲﴾

And those who believe and do good
works and believe in that which is
revealed to Muhammad–and it is the
truth from their Sustainer (Rabb)–
He rids them of their ill deeds and
improves their state.

47:2

وَ الَّذِيْنَ اٰمَنُوْا وَ عَمِلُوا الصّٰلِحٰتِ
وَ اٰمَنُوْا بِمَا نُزِّلَ عَلٰى مُحَمَّدٍ وَّ هُوَ
الْحَقُّ مِنْ رَّبِّهِمْ ۙ كَفَّرَ عَنْهُمْ سَيِّاٰتِهِمْ
وَ اَصْلَحَ بَالَهُمْ ۝٢

This, because they who are bent on denying the truth pursue falsehood, whereas they who have attained to faith pursue (but) the truth (that flows) from their Sustainer. In this way does God set forth unto man the parables of their true state.

47:3

ذٰلِكَ بِاَنَّ الَّذِيْنَ كَفَرُوا اتَّبَعُوا
الْبٰطِلَ وَ اَنَّ الَّذِيْنَ اٰمَنُوا اتَّبَعُوا
الْحَقَّ مِنْ رَّبِّهِمْ ؕ كَذٰلِكَ يَضْرِبُ اللّٰهُ
لِلنَّاسِ اَمْثٰلَهُمْ ﴿۳﴾

Now those who
have attained to
faith say, "Would that
a revelation (allowing us to
fight) was bestowed from on
high!". But now that a revelation
clear in and by itself, mentioning
war, has been bestowed from on
high, thou cannot see those in whose
hearts is disease looking at you, (O
Muhammad,) with the look of one
who is about to faint for fear of death!
And yet, far better for them would be
obedience (to Allah's call) and a word
that could win (His) approval: for,
since the matter has been resolved
(by His Revelation), it would
be but for their own good to
remain true to Allah.

47:20, 21

وَ يَقُوْلُ الَّذِيْنَ اٰمَنُوْا
لَوْلَا نُزِّلَتْ سُوْرَةٌ ۚ فَاِذَآ
اُنْزِلَتْ سُوْرَةٌ مُّحْكَمَةٌ وَّ ذُكِرَ
فِيْهَا الْقِتَالُ ۙ رَاَيْتَ الَّذِيْنَ فِيْ
قُلُوْبِهِمْ مَّرَضٌ يَّنْظُرُوْنَ اِلَيْكَ نَظَرَ
الْمَغْشِيِّ عَلَيْهِ مِنَ الْمَوْتِ ؕ فَاَوْلٰى
لَهُمْ ۚ ﴿٢٠﴾ طَاعَةٌ وَّ قَوْلٌ مَّعْرُوْفٌ ۫
فَاِذَا عَزَمَ الْاَمْرُ ۫ فَلَوْ صَدَقُوا
اللّٰهَ لَكَانَ خَيْرًا لَّهُمْ ۚ ﴿٢١﴾

Will they not, then, ponder over this Quran?–or, are there locks upon their hearts?

47:24

اَفَلَا يَتَدَبَّرُوْنَ الْقُرْاٰنَ اَمْ عَلٰى قُلُوْبٍ
اَقْفَالُهَا ﴿٢٤﴾

Qaf. consider this sublime Quran!

50:1

قٓ قف ج وَ الۡقُرۡاٰنِ الۡمَجِيۡدِ ۚ ﴿۱﴾

In this, behold, there is indeed a reminder for everyone whose heart is wide-awake-that is, everyone who lends ear with a conscious mind.

50:37

إِنَّ فِيْ ذٰلِكَ لَذِكْرٰى لِمَنْ كَانَ لَهٗ قَلْبٌ
أَوْ أَلْقَى السَّمْعَ وَهُوَ شَهِيْدٌ ﴿٣٧﴾

Fully aware are We of what they (who deny resurrection) do say; and you cannot by any means force them (to believe in it). Yet nonetheless, remind them, through this Quran, all those who may fear My warning.

50:45

نَحْنُ اَعْلَمُ بِمَا يَقُوْلُوْنَ وَ مَآ اَنْتَ
عَلَيْهِمْ بِجَبَّارٍ قف فَذَكِّرْ بِالْقُرْاٰنِ مَنْ
يَّخَافُ وَعِيْدِ ﴿٤٥﴾ ع

For, by the Sustainer (Rabb) of heaven and earth, this (life after death) is the very truth–as true as that you are endowed with speech!

51:23

فَوَرَبِّ السَّمَآءِ وَالْاَرْضِ اِنَّهٗ لَحَقٌّ
مِّثْلَ مَآ اَنَّكُمْ تَنْطِقُوْنَ ﴿٢٣﴾ ع

And We have indeed made the Quran easy to understand and remember: then is there any that will receive admonition? (Who will reflect and take advice from it?)

54:17

وَلَقَدْ يَسَّرْنَا الْقُرْآنَ لِلذِّكْرِ فَهَلْ
مِن مُّدَّكِرٍ ﴿١٧﴾

How severe is the suffering which I inflict when My warnings (Quran) are disregarded!

54:21

فَكَيْفَ كَانَ عَذَابِي وَ نُذُرِ ﴿٢١﴾

Hence, indeed, We made this Quran easy to bear in mind: who, then, is willing to take it to heart?

54:32

وَلَقَدْ يَسَّرْنَا الْقُرْآنَ لِلذِّكْرِ فَهَلْ
مِنْ مُّدَّكِرٍ ﴿٣٢﴾

The Most Gracious has imparted this
Quran (unto man).

55:1, 2

اَلرَّحْمٰنُ ۙ﴿۱﴾

عَلَّمَ الْقُرْاٰنَ ؕ﴿۲﴾

Nay, I call to witness the coming-down in parts (of this Quran).

56:75

فَلَآ أُقۡسِمُ بِمَوَٰقِعِ ٱلنُّجُومِ ﴿٧٥﴾

That this is indeed a Quran Most Honourable. In a Book well-guarded, Which none shall touch (in spirit and understanding) but those who are clean.

56:77, 78, 79

اِنَّهٗ لَقُرْاٰنٌ كَرِيْمٌ ﴿۷۷﴾ فِيْ كِتٰبٍ
مَّكْنُوْنٍ ﴿۷۸﴾ لَّا يَمَسُّهٗٓ اِلَّا
الْمُطَهَّرُوْنَ ﴿۷۹﴾

A revelation from the Sustainer (Rabb) of all the worlds! Would you, now, look down with disdain on a tiding like this and make it your daily bread (as it were) to call the truth a lie?

56:80, 81, 82

تَنْزِيْلٌ مِّنْ رَّبِّ الْعٰلَمِيْنَ ﴿٨٠﴾ اَفَبِهٰذَا
الْحَدِيْثِ اَنْتُمْ مُّدْهِنُوْنَ ﴿٨١﴾ وَ
تَجْعَلُوْنَ رِزْقَكُمْ اَنَّكُمْ تُكَذِّبُوْنَ ﴿٨٢﴾

Verily, this is indeed the truth of truths.

56:95

إِنَّ هٰذَا لَهُوَ حَقُّ الْيَقِينِ ﴿٩٥﴾ ج

Is it not time that the hearts of all who have attained to faith should feel humble at the remembrance of God and of all the truth that has been bestowed (on them) from on high,lest they become like those who were granted revelation afore-time, and whose hearts have hardened with the passing of time so that many of them are now depraved?

57:16

اَلَمْ يَاْنِ لِلَّذِيْنَ اٰمَنُوْٓا اَنْ تَخْشَعَ
قُلُوْبُهُمْ لِذِكْرِ اللّٰهِ وَمَا نَزَلَ مِنَ
الْحَقِّ ۙ وَلَا يَكُوْنُوْا كَالَّذِيْنَ اُوْتُوا
الْكِتٰبَ مِنْ قَبْلُ فَطَالَ عَلَيْهِمُ الْاَمَدُ
فَقَسَتْ قُلُوْبُهُمْ ۭ وَكَثِيْرٌ مِّنْهُمْ
فٰسِقُوْنَ ﴿١٦﴾

O you who have attained to faith! Remain conscious of Allah, and believe in His Messenger, (and) He will grant you doubly of His grace, and will kindle for you a light wherein you shall walk, and will forgive you (your past sins): for Allah is Much-Forgiving, a Dispenser of Grace.

57:28

يٰٓاَيُّهَا الَّذِيْنَ اٰمَنُوا اتَّقُوا اللّٰهَ وَ
اٰمِنُوْا بِرَسُوْلِهٖ يُؤْتِكُمْ كِفْلَيْنِ
مِنْ رَّحْمَتِهٖ وَ يَجْعَلْ لَّكُمْ نُوْرًا
تَمْشُوْنَ بِهٖ وَ يَغْفِرْ لَكُمْ ؕ وَاللّٰهُ
غَفُوْرٌ رَّحِيْمٌ ۙ ﴿٢٨﴾

Had We bestowed this Quran from on high upon a mountain, thou wouldst indeed see it humbling itself, breaking asunder for awe of Allah. And all such parables We propound to men, so that they might learn to think.

59:21

لَوْ اَنْزَلْنَا هٰذَا الْقُرْاٰنَ عَلٰى جَبَلٍ
لَّرَاَيْتَهٗ خٰشِعًا مُّتَصَدِّعًا مِّنْ خَشْيَةِ
اللّٰهِ ؕ وَ تِلْكَ الْاَمْثَالُ نَضْرِبُهَا
لِلنَّاسِ لَعَلَّهُمْ يَتَفَكَّرُوْنَ ﴿٢١﴾

Believe, therefore, in Allah and His Messenger, and in the Light (Quran) which We have sent down. And Allah is well acquainted with all that you do.

64:8

فَاٰمِنُوْا بِاللّٰهِ وَ رَسُوْلِهٖ وَ النُّوْرِ
الَّذِیْٓ اَنْزَلْنَا ؕ وَ اللّٰهُ بِمَا تَعْمَلُوْنَ
خَبِیْرٌ ﴿۸﴾

But it is nothing less than a Message
from Allah to all the worlds.

68:52

وَمَا هُوَ اِلَّا ذِكْرٌ لِّلْعٰلَمِيْنَ ﴿۵۲﴾ ع

(it is) a Revelation from the Sustainer (Rabb) of all the worlds. Now if he (whom We have entrusted with it) had dared to attribute some of his own sayings unto Us, We would indeed have seized him by his right hand, and would indeed have cut his life-vein, and none of you could have saved him!

69:43, 44, 45, 46

تَنْزِيْلٌ مِّنْ رَّبِّ الْعٰلَمِيْنَ ﴿٤٣﴾ وَلَوْ
تَقَوَّلَ عَلَيْنَا بَعْضَ الْاَقَاوِيْلِ ﴿٤٤﴾ لا
لَاَخَذْنَا مِنْهُ بِالْيَمِيْنِ ﴿٤٥﴾ لا ثُمَّ لَقَطَعْنَا
مِنْهُ الْوَتِيْنَ ﴿٤٦﴾ صلے

And, surely, this Quran is a
reminder to all the Allah-conscious!
And, behold, well do We know that
among you are such as will give the
lie to it yet, behold, this (rejection)
will indeed become a source of bitter
regret for all who deny the truth of
Allah's Revelation for, verily, it is
truth absolute!

69:48, 49, 50, 51

وَ اِنَّهٗ لَتَذْكِرَةٌ لِّلْمُتَّقِیْنَ ﴿۴۸﴾ وَ اِنَّا
لَنَعْلَمُ اَنَّ مِنْكُمْ مُّكَذِّبِیْنَ ﴿۴۹﴾ وَ اِنَّهٗ
لَحَسْرَةٌ عَلَى الْكٰفِرِیْنَ ﴿۵۰﴾ وَ اِنَّهٗ لَحَقُّ
الْیَقِیْنِ ﴿۵۱﴾

Say: It has been revealed to me
that some of the unseen beings
gave ear (to this Quran), and
thereupon said unto their fellow-
beings: "'Verily, we have heard a
wondrous discourse, guiding towards
consciousness of what is right; and so
We have come to believe in it. And we
shall never ascribe divinity to anyone
beside our Sustainer (Rabb).

72:1, 2

قُلْ اُوْحِیَ اِلَیَّ اَنَّهُ اسْتَمَعَ نَفَرٌ مِّنَ
الْجِنِّ فَقَالُوْٓا اِنَّا سَمِعْنَا قُرْاٰنًا عَجَبًا ۙ﴿١﴾
یَّهْدِیْٓ اِلَی الرُّشْدِ فَاٰمَنَّا بِهٖ ؕ وَلَنْ نُّشْرِكَ
بِرَبِّنَآ اَحَدًا ۙ﴿٢﴾

Or add to it (at will); and (during that time) recite the Quran calmly and distinctly, with your mind attuned to its meaning.

73:4

اَوْ زِدْ عَلَيْهِ وَ رَتِّلِ الْقُرْاٰنَ تَرْتِيْلًا ۭ﴿۴﴾

Surely this is a Reminder (warning): therefore, whoso will, let him take a (straight) path to his Sustainer (Rabb)!

73:19

إِنَّ هٰذِهِۦ تَذْكِرَةٌ ۖ فَمَن شَآءَ ٱتَّخَذَ إِلَىٰ
رَبِّهِۦ سَبِيلًا ﴿١٩﴾

Behold,
(O Messenger,)
your Sustainer (Rabb)
knows that you keep awake
(in prayer) nearly two-thirds of
the night, or one-half of it, or a third
of it, together with some of those who
follow thee. And Allah who determines
the measure of night and day, is aware that
you would never grudge it: and therefore
He turns towards you in His grace. Recite,
then, as much of the Quran as you may do
with ease. He knows that in time there will be
among you sick people, and others who will go
about the land in search of Allah's bounty, and
others who will fight in Allah's cause. Recite,
then, (only) as much of it as you may do with
ease, and be constant in prayer, and spend in
charity,and (thus) lend unto Allah a goodly
loan: for whatever good deed you may offer
up in your own behalf, you shall truly
find it with Allah - better, and richer
in reward. And always seek Allah's
forgiveness: behold, Allah is
much-forgiving, a dispenser
of grace!

73:20

تَيَسَّرَ مِنَ
الْقُرْاٰنِ ؕ عَلِمَ اَنْ
سَيَكُوْنُ مِنْكُمْ مَّرْضٰى ۙ
وَاٰخَرُوْنَ يَضْرِبُوْنَ فِى الْاَرْضِ
يَبْتَغُوْنَ مِنْ فَضْلِ اللّٰهِ ۙ وَاٰخَرُوْنَ
يُقٰتِلُوْنَ فِىْ سَبِيْلِ اللّٰهِ ۖؗ فَاقْرَءُوْا مَا تَيَسَّرَ
مِنْهُ ۙ وَاَقِيْمُوا الصَّلٰوةَ وَاٰتُوا الزَّكٰوةَ وَ
اَقْرِضُوا اللّٰهَ قَرْضًا حَسَنًا ؕ وَمَا تُقَدِّمُوْا
لِاَنْفُسِكُمْ مِّنْ خَيْرٍ تَجِدُوْهُ عِنْدَ
اللّٰهِ هُوَ خَيْرًا وَّ اَعْظَمَ اَجْرًا ؕ
وَاسْتَغْفِرُوا اللّٰهَ ؕ اِنَّ اللّٰهَ
غَفُوْرٌ رَّحِيْمٌ ﴿٢٠﴾ ع

This surely is an Reminder (warning): Let any who will, keep it in remembrance!

74:54, 55

كَلَّآ إِنَّهُۥ تَذۡكِرَةٌ ﴿٥٤﴾ ج

فَمَن شَآءَ ذَكَرَهُۥ ﴿٥٥﴾ ط

Move not your tongue in haste, (repeating the words of the Revelation:) for, behold, it is for Us to gather it (in your heart,) and to cause it to be read (as it ought to be read) Thus, when We recite it, follow thou its wording (with all your mind): and then, behold, it will be for Us to make its meaning clear.

75:16, 17, 18, 19

لَا تُحَرِّكْ بِهٖ لِسَانَكَ لِتَعْجَلَ بِهٖ ؕ ﴿۱۶﴾
اِنَّ عَلَيْنَا جَمْعَهٗ وَ قُرْاٰنَهٗ ۚۖ ﴿۱۷﴾ فَاِذَا
قَرَاْنٰهُ فَاتَّبِعْ قُرْاٰنَهٗ ۚ ﴿۱۸﴾ ثُمَّ اِنَّ عَلَيْنَا
بَيَانَهٗ ؕ ﴿۱۹﴾

This is a warning : Whosoever will, let him take a (straight) Path to his Sustainer (Rabb).

76:29

إِنَّ هَٰذِهِۦ تَذْكِرَةٌ ۖ فَمَن شَآءَ ٱتَّخَذَ إِلَىٰ
رَبِّهِۦ سَبِيلًا ﴿٢٩﴾

Nay, Surely, these (messages) are but a reminder: and so, whoever is willing may remember Him in (the light of His) revelations blest with dignity lofty and pure, (borne) by the hands of messengers noble and most virtuous.

80:11, 12, 13, 14, 15, 16

كَلَّآ اِنَّهَا تَذْكِرَةٌ ۚ ﴿١١﴾ فَمَنْ شَآءَ ذَكَرَهٗ
﴿١٢﴾ فِيْ صُحُفٍ مُّكَرَّمَةٍ ۙ ﴿١٣﴾ مَّرْفُوْعَةٍ
مُّطَهَّرَةٍ ۙ ﴿١٤﴾ بِاَيْدِيْ سَفَرَةٍ ۙ ﴿١٥﴾ كِرَامٍ
بَرَرَةٍ ؕ ﴿١٦﴾

Certainly this is no less than a
Message to (all) the Worlds:

81:27

اِنۡ هُوَ اِلَّا ذِكۡرٌ لِّلۡعٰلَمِيۡنَ ﴿٢٧﴾ لا

And (that), when the Quran is read
unto them, they do not fall down
in prostration?

84:21

وَ اِذَا قُرِئَ عَلَیۡہِمُ الۡقُرۡاٰنُ لَا
یَسۡجُدُوۡنَ ﴿۲۱﴾ السجدة ط

Behold, this (Quran) is indeed a word that between truth and falsehood, and is no idle tale.

86:13, 14

إِنَّهٗ لَقَوۡلٌ فَصۡلٌ ۙ ﴿١٣﴾

وَّ مَا هُوَ بِالۡهَزۡلِ ؕ ﴿١٤﴾

We shall teach you, and you will not forget (aught of what you art taught), save what Allah may will you to forget)–for, surely, He alone knows all that is open to man's perception as well as all that is hidden.

87:6, 7

سَنُقۡرِئُكَ فَلَا تَنۡسٰۤى ﴿٦﴾ اِلَّا مَا شَآءَ
اللّٰهُ ؕ اِنَّهٗ يَعۡلَمُ الۡجَهۡرَ وَ مَا يَخۡفٰى ﴿٧﴾

Read–for thy Sustainer is the Most Bountiful One.

96:3

اِقْرَاْ وَ رَبُّكَ الْاَكْرَمُ ﴿٣﴾ لا

An apostle from God, conveying (unto them) revelations blest with purity, wherein there are ordinances of ever-true soundness and clarity.

98:2, 3

رَسُوۡلٌ مِّنَ اللّٰهِ يَتۡلُوۡا صُحُفًا مُّطَهَّرَةً ۙ﴿۲﴾
فِيۡهَا كُتُبٌ قَيِّمَةٌ ؕ﴿۳﴾